More Praise for Kevin ....g

"In clean lines and tenderly orchestrated sentences Pilkington lets the inconsequentials we mostly live among add up to a life known and accepted, and rendered into an urban lyricism that reminds of Frank O'Hara, cut with a splash of Raymond Chandler."
—**Eamon Grennan**

"In the Eyes of a Dog is a bluesy, belated love song—a little dose of O'Hara and a touch of island music—to the one who abides, the city."
—**David Baker**

"There is a wide and magical sky over these beautifully-conceived and choreographed poems . . ."
—**Carol Muske-Dukes**

"It's thrilling to watch a poet create a world—fascinating when it turns out to be the one we live in."
—**Dennis Nurkse**

"Kevin Pilkington's narratives of daily life are tender and melancholy, lightened with a gentle surreal humor and a steadfast affection for the people and the city he is kin to."
—**Jean Valentine**

Also by Kevin Pilkington

Poetry
Reading Stone (chapbook)
On This Quiet Hill (chapbook)
Getting By (chapbook)
Spare Change
St. Andrew's Head (chapbook)
Ready to Eat the Sky
In the Eyes of a Dog
The Unemployed Man Who Became a Tree

Fiction
Summer Shares (novel)

Where You Want to Be

New and Selected Poems

Kevin Pilkington

Black
Lawrence
Press

Black
Lawrence
Press

www.blacklawrence.com

Executive Editor: Diane Goettel
Cover and Book Design: Amy Freels
Cover Art: Frans Masereel, "Escaliers a Montmarte" © 2014 Artists Rights
Society (ARS), New York / VG Bild-Kunst, Bonn

All new work copyright © 2015 Kevin Pilkington
ISBN: 978-1-62557-927-0

Published 2015 by Black Lawrence Press.
Printed in the United States.

For Jack and Lillian Pilkington

"When we are in love, we love the grass
And the barn, and the lightpoles,
And the small mainstreets abandoned all night."
—Robert Bly

"As I went along my street, which mounts steeply,
I was gripped by a rhythm which took possession
of me and soon gave me the impression of some force
outside myself."
—Paul Valéry

Contents

from In the Eyes of a Dog *(2009)*

from **The Unemployed Man Who Became a Tree** *(2011)*

New Poems

Cannibalism Isn't What It Appears to Be

Cabs are getting too expensive.
One had windshield wipers that kept going
back and forth in time with every song
on the radio. I wasn't impressed and told

the driver don't even think about my paying
extra for it. He turned, looked at me
opened his mouth and let rocks fall out.
I just don't want to waste money and try

to make a little extra wherever I can.
When I didn't need a question mark
at the end of a sentence, I wrote to an
ex-girlfriend, I turned it upside down

until it looked like a saxophone and
pawned it in a shop downtown. I also want
to explain why my hand looks the way it does.
Last winter I was eating a pretzel the same

color as my gloves. By mistake, I bit into
my hand then couldn't finish the pretzel
since I was already full on my thumb
and index finger.

I will never make a mistake like that
again and have become a lot more careful
over the past few months. I have.
I really have.

A Manual for Urban Living

Most things begin here in this city.
When the A train runs uptown
it rattles an orchard in Texas
causing fruit to fall from trees.
And when a glass of beer is knocked
over in a bar on Tenth Avenue the sunset
spills across the sky on the West Coast.
I quickly found out that any street
stretching across town is a kind
of rope that anyone can trip over.
And when I heard a neighbor on
the first floor was found in his
living room hanging from a piece
of Third Avenue wrapped around his neck,
I decided to find out what was hanging
over my head.

On the clearest night I could find,
I took an elevator to the roof
of a high rise then kept going to look
for a piece of moon, a bit of star
anything that resembled the sky
before I moved here. Later I learned
how to say no beginning with a woman
at a party who asked me to get her
a glass of wine. I told her she shouldn't
since she was pregnant. She claimed

she wasn't—the truth was she swallowed
the world. After she walked away,
I just hoped whenever her water broke
it turned out to be the Atlantic.

Healthcare

Everything keeps changing
that's why I like to walk around
uptown—it has looked the same
for years and most buildings
resemble Cole Porter.

I haven't been sleeping much
and now keep my eyes in bags
so I won't lose them. Last week
I heard music coming from a jazz
club I walked by. Tired as usual,
I tripped over a horn solo knocking
a few notes on to the street a car ran over.

I just need things to slow down
and plan to bring the next year
to the nearest church since nothing
moves slower than a sermon
and ask the priest to place it in
his next on Sunday.

I used to tell the women I slept with
that they should wear high heels
when we were together. It was really
another way to deal better with the curves
life sent my way. I've grown since then
and now tell them to keep wearing
those stilettos since the air is cleaner
up there and better for their health.

And I've discovered what it means
to be passionate and committed—
it happens when I go to the park
on the West Side that is big enough
for drugs but thankfully too small for rape.
When I walk through its dry leaves
they sound like a rustling fire,
and I make sure to keep walking
until I burst into flames.

The Other Guy in the Song

"So make it one for my baby
And one more for the road"
—Johnny Mercer/Harold Arlen

I'm sitting at the far end of a bar
in a tavern on Third having a beer
before meeting a friend uptown in about
an hour. At the center of the bar sits a thin
guy around fifty in a gray suit and fedora—
the kind of hat all guys wore in those forties
black and white movies—resting on the back
of his head. He was here when I walked in
to get out of the rain that has finally stopped.
Now it's dark out and neon lights from store
windows and signs are smeared across the street
like mascara on the face of a woman
who just stopped crying.

The guy in the suit between sips of his drink
talks to the bartender he calls Joe even though
his name is Nick and slurs, it's a quarter
to three nobody in the place except you and me.
It's really a quarter to six in the evening
and he is too far gone to notice me. When Nick
walks to the other end of the bar, the guy keeps
talking into his glass about losing his girlfriend,
how awful he feels, then downs the glass and orders
another for her, his baby, and one more for the road.

He keeps talking and starts to raise his voice
about putting a nickel in the machine,
the jukebox near the door and play
sad songs to match how bad he feels.
Before he begins to annoy me, I remember
how it feels and what he's going through. The last
woman I lived with one night told me
she was going out to buy a bottle of wine.
I didn't realize the liquor store would be in Paris.
So I decide to help him out even if I can't recall
any song costing a nickel. I take two quarters
from my pocket, go over to the jukebox and find
BB King and Joe Williams.

As I pass him going back to my seat,
his hat falls off; I pick it up with both hands
as if it were a plate with a steak on it
and place it next to him on the bar. He glances
at me, says he's a poet with a lot to say, then
turns back to his drink. No poet could ever
afford the suit he is wearing. He mumbles
he'll leave soon since Nick must be anxious
to close. I almost tell him to relax, nothing
is closing for at least another eight hours.

I see its time to leave and meet my friend
uptown, pay for my beer and as I walk past
him, he looks at me claiming again he has a lot
to say but has to be true to some code.
I gently pat him on the back, hope he gets home
safely and walk outside. I stand near the curb,
the air hasn't felt this good for a long time.

For some reason I feel better than I did an hour ago
so I take a deep breath filling my lungs with all
the midtown they can hold. In fact I feel even healthier,
stronger and to prove it I stop the next cab that comes by
with nothing more than lifting my right arm.

Viagra

I walk to the end of the block to get a better
look at the river. Where the sun reaches for waves
diamonds float. A tug slowly pushes a barge
scattering some as others rattle towards the river's bank.
Gulls flutter and slide over the tug's bow
like the whitecaps waves lost in strong winds.

The apartment across the way is how people
walk on other peoples' heads without falling off.
The building in back of it is as tall as I am
since we stand eye to roof. I just signed a new
lease to my apartment for another year
and had to write my name in black ink
making it look like the New York skyline at night.
The factory to the left must be manufacturing
Viagra to keep its smoke stack erect for so long
without going limp.

I realize this is not a view for everyone.
That's why I'm taking it to the diner two blocks
over and ask the cook who I know to place
it on the menu in between the pork chops and brisket
so anyone can see it's one of the day's specials.

Francine Peron on Ice

I bought an old piano from the guy
in the apartment above mine
after I got him to throw the black keys
in for free. I tried playing it by ear
but kept hurting the side of my head.
I'm thinking of taking lessons.

There's a playground with a skating
rink on Seventh. It reminded me
when I was a kid in first grade
how I fell on the one near my home
and the way Francine Peron skated
around me giggling as I crawled off.
My face was red as the skirt around
her waist that flared out like an umbrella.
After that there was no way I could
ask her to marry me the next day
in recess like I planned. Years later
another girl laughed at me but I made sure
I wasn't on all fours or anywhere near
thin ice.

Ever since I heard a friend of mine
jumped from a bridge near Spokane
so he wouldn't have to show up for work
on Monday, I won't fly west and only
take part-time jobs. Except for all
the noise: clouds rubbing against sky,
cats walking, the war taking place inside

the novel on my desk, cold beers losing
their heads in the bar on the corner,
I like it here. And I don't let things
get to me the way they once did.
When my ex wrote to say the weeping
willow in back of the place we shared
stopped crying as soon as I left
and has never looked better, I admit
it bothered me for a few minutes.
Only a few.

Flu Shot

I try not to look at the woman
walking towards me but her shirt
is no bigger than a bandage and
her heels are so high she might need
an oxygen tank rather than the suitcase
on wheels she pulls behind her.
I just hope the two assholes she
is walking next to aren't with her.
The guy on her right is in a suit
and wears a toupee that looks
like a black squirrel fell off a tree,
landed on his head and didn't
survive the fall. He's talking to the guy
next to him with hair plugs resembling the hair
on the head of Chatty Cathy the doll
my sister dragged everywhere when she
was a kid. Maybe I'm just pissed off
my arm is aching. I only left
the doctor's office ten minutes ago
after getting a flu shot. I hate needles
and this one looked like the Empire
State Building; when he injected it
I could feel at least seventy floors
enter my arm. No wonder it feels so heavy.
Then for some reason discovering
there was a couple of hundred bucks
in my bank account when I thought
it empty; seeing a Hopper canvas
for the first time or hearing

the Clifford Brown with Strings
CD is how I felt seeing the girl
with the bandage end up standing next to me.
Even her taking out a cigarette as we
waited for the light to change couldn't
diminish the moment. Of course
I didn't notice how the smoke slid
out of her mouth or the way it
sounded rubbing up against a breeze,
perhaps the way that skirt of hers
might, slowly sliding down her legs.

Snow in San Diego

The women who walk along
Eighth Ave. have hips that move
back and forth like bells.
The new church going up
in the middle of the block
should place a few in its steeple
so when they ring every noon
it will sound like heaven.

Each morning I stop
in the diner where pigeons
sleep out front like a flock
of bocce balls the Italian guys
used to play in the park all day.

With suntan lotion on and dark
glasses, I always order the breakfast
special, look down at the sunny side up
eggs, then close my eyes to work
on a tan so when I leave even if it snows
the city feels like San Diego.

Watching Pigeons Eat the Last Five Years

You are sitting on the beach next to the bay
when a pigeon lands near your feet.
You recognize it from back home and guess
it couldn't handle another snowstorm
either and came down here to get away
for the rest of the winter. It used to sit
in front of your building on the sidewalk
looking more like a ball a kid lost resting
near the curb. Now it looks relaxed, cleaner
with tan feathers and has the moves
of a good-looking gull.

There were other pigeons you recognized
in a town whose name you can't remember
but on a local map it is no more than ten
to fifteen inches north of here. They were
standing on and around a Roman statue
of a woman built in Tallahassee.
She is slender with the type of curves
found on dangerous roads, the roads you always
travel and feel at home on. She is the kind of woman
you should go after, even with a heart of concrete,
no arms could be a plus and make things easier.
Even if all the pigeons aren't from back home
it still means they have little use for their wings
or rarely use them and depend on handouts.

The next time you passed through you brought
a bag of crumbs, all that was left of the last
five years. It was all in there: the months you spent
training so you could make the leap from Chet Baker
to Miles Davis; the night you found out locking
the windows and bolting the door wasn't safe sex;
the year your luck got better when you looked
down at the floor into a shattered mirror
and your face stared back like a Picasso portrait;
and the morning you knew a relationship was worth saving
since there could never be anything as sexy as Peggy Lee's voice.
So after emptying the bag, you stamped your foot twice
making sure those pigeons were full on every scrap
and crumb of those five years, until each month, week
and day flew away and you'd never have to reexamine or learn
anything from them again.

If Phone Booths Come Back Superman Will Follow

I take the train from Grand Central
to work each weekday. Track forty
is just past the wall lined with pay
phones that have turned yellow,
afraid they will be removed since
everyone uses a cell these days. No wonder
crime has gone up across the city
now that there are no phone booths
on the streets for Clark Kent to change in.

When a piece of furniture rests against
a wall for years then is removed, it often leaves
behind a dark stain. Where the tracks
curve before 125th Street I can look back
at the city—that's what I see: two dark
stains where the World Trade Center
once leaned against a wall of sky for over
thirty years.

As we go over the Harlem River
two boys heave a large rock into
the water, smashing open a small
wave. When the hole doesn't close
they run and I turn to flip through
a magazine someone left behind.
The train takes an alternate route

through Scotland and a small town
near Glasgow before making another
stop in Fleetwood, the town where I grew up.

I put down the magazine and notice
my parents' car parked once again
near the curb. It's the red Chevy
shaped like a tongue, the one they often
picked me up in when I came back to visit.
I check the time as they get out
and stand by the car. I run to the door
that slides open—after the last passenger
gets on I lean out.

They are smiling and waving for me
to get off. I hold up my wrist, point
to my watch and call out saying I can't
and will be late for work. They
hear me for a change and nod their heads.
They have been retired for awhile
and I would like to catch up, know what
they do to keep busy. Does mom still
cook, and is it low-fat? Is dad
still emotional and has he found
another hobby besides yelling? Before
the door slides shut, I wave—watch
as they get back in the car. I miss them.
They have been dead for over fifteen years.
I'll get off one of these days but not
now. No. Not yet.

On Learning I will Need a New Crown to Replace the One that Should Have Lasted Another Ten Years

My dentist told me I'll need
a new crown for the last tooth
on the lower left. It's expensive—
the price of the bed I was going
to buy for the new apartment I just
moved into. So for the next few months
I guess I'll just have to sleep in my mouth.

Einstein's Hair

I walk past trees where leaves
are turning white and will look
like Einstein's hair for the next two
weeks before falling off. Across the street
in front of the hospital animal activists
picket holding up signs like large
lollipops protesting the killing of lab animals.

I get it, I really do. Nothing should
be killed not even rodents. It's just
that when I see dark country roads
too dangerous to travel on at night,
they have no business being on the faces
of children leaning over in wheelchairs
their parents pushing them looking
tired, shoulders sloping over like
a question mark at the end of a sentence.

If I were in the lab searching for a cure
so these kids could jump up and run
towards a world that begins with fun
and ends with ice cream instead
of being wheeled back to their hospital rooms,
I'd kill every lab mouse and rat I could
get my hands on. And if you are one
of those who doesn't get it, this is what
I mean. I love dogs.

I'd pick up that cute puppy that just sat
like a cashew, the same puppy that slows everyone
who walks by and smiles down at him and if
there was something in his blood that would
save even one child, I would gut him from throat
to belly to tail to find it.

1942

I didn't know I'd walk into
a movie from the early forties.
It's the only way to explain
entering a restaurant and finding
myself in a tux, with hair slicked
back and shiny as the dance floor
where couples are moving to
the Glenn Miller orchestra with Miller
himself conducting Moonlight Serenade
in a brief cameo.

Cameras are rolling in different
corners of the room then one points
at me with props or a high ball
in my hand as I take a drag on
a cigarette I've never smoked. Women
wear dresses with shoulders
like airstrips, expect for the Lana Turner
look-a-like in a long gown poured
over her like maple syrup, any guy
in an audience will want to lick off,
that is held up with straps the size
of the strings on the violins playing
over any noise in the room,
proving she is my co-star.

I invite her to have a drink with me
at a small table the size of a quarter.
I've never been this confident with a woman
like her—the screenwriter makes sure I am

and I wish he could write my dialogue
when filming is over. I do know
I can't say what I want since
the censor will keep us in our clothes
and out of bed.

I get fed up and begin to improvise,
tell her I'd see her around,
take a drag on my cigarette that is so deep
and fast it misses my lungs,
then crush it into the ashtray
like the front of a car hitting a wall.
She looks up hurt and confused,
as I turn making sure Bogart or
Cagney couldn't do it better and walk
out the door—the biggest badass
on film for 1942.

Outside I am back in my jeans
and sweater and a little confused.
Two guys walking past talk war
and I think we have to stop Hitler,
then remember it is a new war
and the Taliban this time. As I turn
onto my block, I stop to look
at the sun setting over the Hudson.
The sky with those bright colors
and a few clouds perfectly placed
behind it make even a man
like me who doesn't believe in much
of anything admit it must have been
created by the special effects crew and cost
the movie studio a fortune.

Walking Through an Old Photo

I stop in front of a wine store
on First Avenue and stare at an old photo
from 1910 hanging over an expensive
bottle of Burgundy. I lean in closer
to get a better look at the same spot
where I'm standing and the tenements
lining both sides of the street.
They are all no higher than five stories,
one more than I read last weekend.
There is a blacksmith shop where a small
grocery is now and horse shoes hanging
from a wire like flags at a grand opening.
Cars and trucks shaped like boxes
are parked in mounds of vanilla ice cream,
the way snow looked ten years after the turn
of the century. Without all the high rises
there is a lot more sky and St. Monica
who didn't believe in reincarnation will
come back anyway as a church on
79th Street but not for another forty years.

To get an even closer look, I enter
the photo and stroll uptown. The smudge
that was in the middle of the street
walks towards me until it becomes
a man in a long black coat, derby
and a scarf wrapped around his neck
like a pet snake. The large apartment
buildings I always pass are missing with more

tenements in their place. Smoke comes
out of roofs from wood-burning stoves,
making the air smell more like Vermont
than the city. A horse drawn wagon carries
boxes and another is filled with rags.
On 86th Street stores have German names,
butcher shop windows are stuffed with hams,
and rabbits hanging upside down who look
like they may wake and run out the doors,
buckets are stuffed with sauerkraut spilling
over the tops like hay. I keep walking past
breweries, stables and piano factories.

It's getting cold and I decide to take the subway
home—walk past young boys in knickers
throwing snowballs and a cop standing
on the corner with a club in his hand
and a hat shaped like a bell. Across from him
is the El on Second I never knew existed nor
the Harlem Railroad on Lex. I do remember
the subway won't be built for another few years.
I stop in a café on Third and since there is nothing
to go, I sit at a small table near the window.
A waitress in a dress so long it sweeps the floor
like a broom as she walks—her white blouse
is tight fitting until it puffs out as if she is balancing
a soccer ball on each shoulder.

After I order a coffee I realize I feel lost
in my own neighborhood and need to get back
to where this photo began and walk out of it.
I'd be back in this very spot tomorrow

when this café becomes a Radio Shack again.
I'll be buying a new cell phone in less
than twenty-four hours from now and
one hundred years later.

Espresso

The palm trees along the beach
are tall as models on the cover
of *Vogue* but could use more
hairspray to control their palms.
And like any good host the ocean
never runs out of waves and
keeps them coming.

At night I've never seen so many
stars and the Little Dipper looks
a little bigger. Even lights from
fishing boats are just more stars
floating on water.

Every night the moon is shaped
like a slice of lemon floating
in a cup of espresso I ordered
in a café on a street too thin
for the heavy woman walking
with a basket of fruit on her head.
I haven't been able to sleep and figure
it must be from gazing up
at all that caffeine filled with twilight.

Watching a Plane Through a Bone

I got out of the city for a few days
and I'm now on a trail in Vermont
that's as narrow as the ledge birds
sit on over a bodega near Fourth Street.
I just passed fur trees and hope no one
from PETA comes up to throw paint
on them. I reach a clearing and get a good
look at the sky that today is as clear
as any song Ben Webster blows through
his sax, then down at the valley that should
be drab and weathered after being kept
outside all winter. Perhaps someone
like my grandmother got down on her hands
and knees the way the old-timers did it
and scrubbed and polished every tree, stone
and stream until they shined. As I head on,
I see a small deer hop into the bushes
as if its legs had springs in them and for a second
think of Bambi then realize this isn't a path
I can stay on it now that it turned into the quickest
way back to my childhood. Over to the side
of it is a left over patch of snow that can't
be used again next winter and nearby is a small
white bone. I pick it up, try to guess
what kind of animal once covered it, notice
the center is hollow, then hold it up
like a telescope to examine the sky. I find
a plane no bigger than a nickel and follow it
until it reaches a mountain range
and is finally swallowed up by rock.

A Heartfelt Thank You to All the Women Who Dumped Me

I want to thank them all
for finding fault with me,
pointing out my imperfections
then ending it in person, by phone
and even by email.

To Claudia who fifteen years ago
learned in time to despise me
for snoring and sleeping with the window
open even in winter. And Margot
who was quite tall and during
the first few months said I was the perfect
height for her but discovered my salary
was way too small. Then there was Kate
who was in love with David Bowie and even
though she tried could only love me.

So thanks to each and every one
for making sure I wasn't worth it.
If things had worked out
with any of them, I would never
have met you.

Our anniversary is coming soon.
Even though you say you want
nothing since what we have between us
is gift enough, I plan to go to the shore

at midnight, remove as many stars as I can hold
before rearranging the rest so no one
will notice they are gone. Then I'll place
a dozen or more stars attached to long
stems of sky in the glass vase shaped
like hands at the center of our table filled
with a glittering bouquet of twilight.

Maggots

In this high-tech age
of medical advancement
doctors have gone retro
and found maggots to clean
infected wounds with no
patient discomfort. Those
same tiny insects that look
like pedestrians moving along
the streets if you look down
from a plane. Or more like rice
when thrown outside church
at a bride and groom.

With a history of rotting
meat and horror films
where they work as extras
crawling in and out
of the eyes of a corpse,
it's difficult to accept their new
role as healers. But *The New England
Journal of Medicine* is pleased
with their work and hospitals have opened
maggot obedience training schools.
So after they nibble on scabs
and pus, are full on thighs or burping
up pieces of elbow, they know
enough to stop when told and never
eat towards bone.

Fetch

The block association fought
to stop the high rise going up
on the corner of Fifty-ninth and Third.
The contractor won and didn't care
he would have to tear down
historic tenements along with the one
I lived in or obstruct the views
of residents who lived there for years.
I was forced to move uptown
and now looking at it from thirty
blocks away it has become no bigger
than a stick. So I reach down
and snap off the top, bring it to the park
and play fetch with my dog. I heave
it as far as I can and he runs after
it, his thick coat black and shiny
in the sun—making the woman walking
by in a fur coat jealous. He runs back
towards me with at least twenty floors
clenched in his teeth, shaking his head
back and forth with condos breaking
off and falling on the grass. At least
five fall around my feet, into broken
pieces of greed as I kneel, pat his head
and say: good dog, good dog.

Long as a Quart of Milk

Once I undressed a tree,
got a splinter in my thumb
and decided that was it
for one-night stands.

The woman next door who
dresses in clothes that make her
look like the English countryside
keeps yelling at her son
about being spoiled.

I wish I could help him,
tell her of course he's spoiled
it's hot out so she should keep
him in a room with the AC on.
It would keep him fresh longer
or at least as long as a quart of milk.

I rent a small studio in the tenement building
next door that looks like Lou Reed.
I've lived here for awhile and have no plans
of moving. There really isn't any point now
that I know this neighborhood so well I can
recite any street by heart to anyone
who will listen.

It's Early

The East River hasn't begun to moan yet and already
my hands are shaking.
I keep them in my pockets just to remind myself
with so much out of reach
they are still worth the spare change they are holding on to.

I've lived in this city for years so when tourists pass me
on the sidewalk speaking another language
I can translate every word I hear. When someone walks by
speaking English, I don't understand much anymore.

There is a song I heard on the radio this morning
I can't stand that is stuck in my head.
I make sure to keep my mouth shut in case someone
walks too close,
I don't want them to hear the accordion.

An older Italian man with cameras hanging from his neck
like Olympic gold medals
and an accent so heavy it could lose a couple of pounds says to a friend
that a bagel is a hole with dough around it.

I stop in a deli, order a Danish covered in sugar
as if it were dipped in smoke,
sit at the counter next to the window and with a cup of coffee
look like I joined the police force.

I eat quickly since I'm late for work again and wish
the days were longer
that happy-hour had another 20 minutes and there were still
four Beatles left instead of two.

Back on the corner waiting for the light to change
a construction worker drills
into the concrete as if he were the last dentist
in the city.

Dust floats over with no understanding that even
a breeze has a cost
or when it leans against me that I'm not, absolutely not the one
who can be counted on for anything.

Fishing Out the Moon

I told her I could change and
of course I would stop cursing.
I just needed to fucking convince
her this time.

She wants me to turn my life
over to Jesus. No problem. I was already
halfway there and use his name
every time I get pissed off.

Landing a 9 to 5 job wouldn't be difficult
either, it's just that I like working
for myself, creating my own hours
collecting empty bottles from trash cans

and cashing them in isn't easy.
Maybe she is right—it might be
time to look for a job with a steady
paycheck and benefits.

What I won't do anymore is when
we are on the roof and she finds
the moon floating in her drink.
I'll leave it there, not try to fish it

out or ruin the rest of the evening
drying it off then looking for a spot
to hang it back up. Last night
when I looked in her wine and saw

it with that frozen smile on its fat face
I had to go look for nails and by
the time I climbed up on the step
ladder, dawn was already at my ankles

and the sun was making its move.
So I don't care what she says
the next time she finds it in her wine or
anything else she might be drinking

I'm just going to leave it there and tell her
to drink around it. I don't care how mad
she gets, I'm not going to do it—
I'm not.

Looking in the Mirror

I order coffee and sit at the counter
next to the window to drink it.
Looking in the cup, I notice the top
floor of the apartment building across
the street. The rent floating with it
tastes rather bitter, so I just add
more sugar. An old man walking by
stops and looks at me, his hair
is the color of the religion in the brick
church on the next block and the lines
on his face are the kind a junkie would snort off
his forehead. He sticks his tongue out
then walks on. I don't blame him
since it's never easy to stare
into the face of a stranger and not see
the resemblance to your own.

from

Spare Change

(1997)

Breakfast

You take a seat
at a table
in a diner on Third
and order breakfast
from a waiter with tattoos
who trained his arms
to keep the eagles on them
from flying away.

You pour cream in your coffee
and by mistake
stir it the color of a woman you forgot
then gulp it down
to forget her all over again.

When the waiter brings a refill,
you keep it black
to make sure
this cup you'll want to drink
instead of kiss.

The weather report over the radio
doesn't predict the salt you shake like snow
over scrambled eggs the color of cabs.
Car horns outside
make you pick up your knife,
lean out the window,
and dip it into the street
to spread some traffic jam across your toast,
and to help rush hour along.

After you finish,
you walk out onto the sidewalk
and look at the city.
It's gray,
the color of ash on a good cigar.

So you reach over your head
rip off some sky,
roll it and light up
then head across town
blowing the rest of the day
into smoke rings
you can stick
your finger through.

Magis

(Watch Hill, Rhode Island)
—for my father

The Ocean House Hotel
looks too big for the hill
it's been sitting on
for the past one hundred years,
but lets the roof sag
like the spine of an old
plow horse, so it can squeeze
in between July and August.

On the patio, I take a seat,
order a drink from a waitress
with icing on her nose and watch
a ferry drag
a long white ribbon out
to Block Island, a piece
of land that looks
shorter than my arm
but with a bit more muscle.

I have a great view
of the coast, spreading
its shoreline open like a lover
the ocean can't seem
to get enough of.
Sailboats are pushovers
for wind and the Montauk

lighthouse keeps blinking
with something caught
in its beam.

Years later, the waitress
brings over my drink
that's strong but still weaker
than the sun. As I take
another sip I see my father
walk up from the beach
where umbrellas grow like
mushrooms in the sand.

He's leaning on his cane
the way all of us
have leaned on him for years.
His right side stiff
from last year's stroke,
each step a limp.
I wave until he sees
me, then wait and help
him into the chair next to mine.
I ask if he wants something
to drink. He shakes his head
no since most of his speech
was lost and now there are
new words and sounds he knows
I have never heard before,
and only my mother can translate.

As he stares out at the view,
I realize for the first time
that I admire this stretch of coast
because it has the look I have always
found in my father's eyes.
It has something to do
with the acceptance of water—
the forgiveness of sand and stone.

We both sit quietly. After
a few moments, I say,
Beautiful, isn't it Dad.
He turns to look at me,
nods his head, smiles and says,
Magis, and I smile back
knowing exactly what he means.

In A Bar on 2nd

You sit in a bar on 2nd Ave.
with a woman you want
but notice the distance
in her eyes has the extra
mile that even another drink
could never help you reach.

Ashes eat slowly down a cigarette
towards her fingers, the way
you would if she'd just take you home
later and let you burn.

She stares at the band
and at the guitar player
who heats the blues with his riffs.

When the drummer slides his brushes
across the snare, it reminds
you how you slid through
the last few years, how most
nights weren't worth the dark
it took to get through them
and each time dawn was the prize,
you turned it down then held on
to your sweat instead.

Now you want to tell this woman
that life is shorter than her skirt,
without its style. As soon as

the next song ends, you want to begin
over with her, learn to love the way
she tilts her head every time she whispers
and be gentle with her body, that up
to now has only kept you thirsty.

When two guys in the next booth
get louder, you consider taking
them on to prove your strength,
but know the only thing you want
to lick tonight are her legs.

After another drink, you realize
that even if she doesn't
need you, there is a lot to be thankful
for: the way your eyes have begun
to blur and how the horn player,
with the good lip, in the last
song of the night, blows your past clean.

The Reincarnation of Montana

—for Uncle John

At a party under
a night that was clear
and moon, my uncle
stood in between jokes,
a brandy glass sitting
its fat rear in his large paw.

He claimed after he went
he would wait seven days
then return. We laughed,
then buried him last week.

He went to a ball.
Bigger than Montana,
he never dressed to die
only to kill. When the last
dance began his heart stopped.
The whole state fell
to the floor in a red jacket.

I went walking last night
and realized for the first time
that I'm not that big,
perhaps a bit shorter
than life.

After reaching the trees
that cricket when the sun drops,
I spotted a bear in the sky
made of stars.
Although it took eight days,
it was good to see
my uncle again.

Buying a Paper

You pass an alley
where a drunk holds
on to a rope of piss
he made with cheap wine
and these streets are the stink
August heats until
your one good lung turns
into a trash can rattling
each time you cough.

Like most tenants you keep
windows open hoping
the sax player on the corner
has a good enough lip tonight
to cool off the next breeze.

Things haven't been right
but you know the voices you hear now
are no longer Irish arguing
in these tenements. After
moving uptown, the problems
they forgot to pack turned Spanish.

Before ever reaching
the newsstand you decided
the past year is worth the 50
cents a paper costs if it has an article
on why the women in your life
never meant more than rent.

Finding none, you light up
a cigarette, sucking down
all the smoke it takes to cloud
reasons why love has meant
just so many trout lying on their side
in the fish market window
with prices on their heads.

Directions Through a Changing Scene

You will pass a field
where corn scratches sky
each wind. Back when fins
meant cars not sharks, nearby
beaches began to resort
for the money farmer and fish
once brought. Dunes mean
motels now, so keep going until
you see sand then turn
left. On your right is a park
where lions guard the gates
roaring louder than stone.
Across from them is a tree
knocked down by a storm,
named after a woman, jealous
of birch. Then you will enter
a town built by whales
chased by fisherman for months,
until each man cursed his ship
and prayed for what was ever
warm on land. After passing
the diner where eggs sizzle
the sun up every morning,
turn on to the road that goes
through a tunnel of trees
its roof made of branches
and leaves and patched
with clouds. Keep traveling
through until you run out

of oak, then when sky breaks
open my house is on the left
sitting in shade if noon is on time.
But if you believe in water
travel on until you reach the ocean,
and watch the waves crash
with enough faith to convince
anyone that you can always
turn around and go home
the way you came.

Going for a Ride

My brother, Tom, picks me up
at the train station in his '67
Austin Healy. He had it painted
the same color red as the lips
of a woman on the train I would
have married if she hadn't gotten off
at the last stop. We decided to take
the car for a spin as he starts
the engine that sounds like a machine
gun, then shoot our way out
of the parking lot.

We head for the coast since spring
is early, but realize April is late
when the breeze coming off the water
is still cooler than James Dean.
Tom turns onto the first road
inland as I turn on the radio
and into an old Stones song that reminds
me of my first girlfriend who really
liked me but loved Mick Jagger.

I switch to another station
where the DJ asks when are we
going to settle down. Tom flips off
the radio and sounding pissed says,
"It's none of that fucker's business."
A few moments later we admit
we'd like to have kids soon;

if they are boys, at least as smart
as our nephew who at age two
already knows most food you eat
and the rest you wear on your head.

We pass a village with homes as white
as any religion I've ever tried
and given up on. In the middle of it
is a tree shaped like an ice cream cone
letting a few buds drip onto
a green napkin of lawn every time
the wind licks.

Tom smiles and says, "It's not like
where we grew up." I tell him
I passed through our hometown
last month and it hasn't change
much. Where the A&P used to be
there's a parking lot that was empty
except for a truck in frozen foods.
The pizza shop is still open
but now a slice costs a pie.
And Mom may be right about
reincarnation. Mr. Miller, our
Phys. Ed. teacher, died in a car crash
three years ago but came back
as the high school gym with his name
over the door.

We decide to go back
to my brother's place; I turn
the radio on again and into some jazz.

I realize we know these country roads
pretty well, then get lost in a Miles Davis
tribute before finding the road we need.
After passing the small white church
that sits like a swan next to a pond,
we are both feeling pretty empty.
So Tom pulls into the first gas station
we find, turns off the engine
and tells the guy at the pump
to fill it up.

A Christmas Poem

I want you back
in the chair by the window
sliding off your stockings
with the moon looking down
grinning at each peak of thigh.

On the couch I lie watching you
my clothes in a heap
near the jazz our stereo tries
cooling us with.

As you walk towards me
high on your heels
your hips sway with that tune,
the one I always swallowed
and never learned to hum.

Show me once more
how you filled my hands
with a purpose I never found
standing, and why quiet groans
worth keeping can never
be touched with tongues.

The slide of your lips on mine
keeps the distance between us moist.
So come back and slowly

move your fingertips up my legs
until I am hard again
with the passion of stone.

Besides, Christmas is in two
days and it looks like snow.

From the Roof

Rain makes streets
shine like the gifted child
you plan on having
with the next woman
who won't let you go.

You can make out
a church that lost
its steeple to fog
and St. James
to the neon sign over
the hotel three blocks away.

A ghost climbs
out of a factory smokestack
on 9th, grabs
the first wind it can
and heads uptown
to haunt lungs.

You notice the river
is still wet from the storm
last week, and know
today's rain will just give
the tide another excuse
to get high again.

To help the congestion on 8th,
you lean over
pull off a line of cars
that looks like adhesive tape
then stick it on a cloud
moving in the same direction
across town.

As soon as you watch them float
out of sight,
a truck parks in front
of your building
right below your chin
with its radio turned up.
But by the time Elvis
reaches you, he thins
into Gershwin.

Over to the right,
you can see the fish market
that closed when the river
turned brown and old tires
became the biggest haul.
The main catch now
are the whores who sway
in front of it, even if there isn't
any wind.

Before you turn
to look uptown,
a customer walks over to one

to see what's caught
in her fish nets before
reaching into his pocket to buy
an hour or two by the pound.

When Iowa was Washed Away with Milk

—for my sister

I put down my book
to watch the snow falling
in the backyard.
It started an hour ago
but is already deeper
than Keats.

Downstairs Maureen is baking—
the kitchen, oven-warm
and cookie-stuffed. I joke
the white spot on her nose is snow
not flour then sit and wait
for the first batch.

After Sinatra, the radio
warns blizzard and I'm warned
to take just one.
I choose an oatmeal shaped
like Iowa, first nibbling
on the northern end of the state
until it cools then chomp south.

When I reach a raisin
that must be Des Moines,
I wash what's left of the state
down with a glass of milk
and begin eyeing Colorado.

Holding a Farm in Your Hand

My brother invited
me and my parents
to his house in Vermont.
I was up early
to see how a flock
of geese pulled in dawn,
rubbed it against mountain peaks
until it sparked sky
and burned away dark.

By seven, the fires
we started crackle
the house warm
and my mother
is at the stove
scrambling the sun
out for good.

My dad is outside
in his favorite sweater
with the large holes
a moth left after
it got full on elbows.
He's walking out
to the pond
he wants to stock,
in front of the house.
At first he thought
pike but now he talks perch.

Tom who jogs a few
miles every morning
is already back
from five but jokes
he is still not stronger
than the coffee I perked.
He had to cut it weak
with cream he bought
from a farm in Manchester,
the same one we spotted
from the side of a mountain
we hiked up last year.

I remember now
looking down at it in a valley,
how I leaned over
to pick up the entire farm
in my hand and for a few
moments, let cows graze
on my thumb.

On this Quiet Hill

(Ireland)
—for my father

On this quiet hill
you can hear
a stray English cloud
move into the next
county a King named
after his third wife.
Here wind must be nobility
since the grass bows
with each gust.

Where prayers fade
into mist over hills,
stone walls quilt
a blanket of farms
and the mountain
just west of the oak
that leans towards Dublin
is filled with streams
and legend.

Near its foot is a cottage
neighbors helped
a farmer thatch
in between pints.

Just to the right
of his barn
is a tower the Saxons
left behind for sheep

to rule, until cattle
snuck in one night
200 years ago and took
it by herd.

Grandpa

Grandpa Joe never worried
about being out of work
since he could always
drink himself into the best
jobs Dublin had to offer.
When he came home from pubs,
he'd hit his wife until
he was sober—the same woman
who has stared for seventy years
with my father's eyes
from the photo in our den.
She died thin and diabetic
a year before the pig
in their barn could have saved
her with the insulin in its pork.

Instead, Joe cut its throat
and boiled bacon to feed
the wake. When the last
mourners whispered good-bye
or slurred his wife saint,
and when he couldn't scare
her back, he gulped another pint
and cursed her on her way.
As his son put him to bed,
Joe hit his wife in the face
one last time. The next
morning, his boy's right eye
was a black stone.

In a month a cousin from America
sent for his son. Joe brought
him to the docks, the day after
a freighter, full to its hull
in wine, sank off the coast.
Waves banged into each other,
some broke spilling foam—
the tide high and still drunk
on cargo. The sight made
Joe's throat go dry. He put
his boy on the ship and headed
for the nearest pub.

Later when he stumbled
into the cottage
and there was no one left
to hit, he went over
to kick his hound, making sure
whenever it dozed, it dreamed boots.

My Father's Hands

When I was six wind
kept blowing my hats off
until my father placed his hand
gently on my head whenever
we crossed the street,
a perfect fit of fingers and palm—
a hat no gust could take from me.

And I remember him placing
his hands on my shoulders
the first time he showed me
a map of Ireland.
He explained how he left there
when he was my age
then pointed to dots,
the same size as the ones
on his hands, that were named
after cities. It was easy
to see even then, if he stayed
he became too large a man
to fit into a country so small.

When we walked into
the funeral home last week
to view my father
for the first time, my mother
hurried over to him, fell
on her knees, buried her head
against the coffin and began

sobbing. As I walked over
to place my arm around her,
I looked into the open casket
and knew there must
have been a mistake.
It wasn't him.

This man's mouth drooped
the way my father's never had
and he was pale, almost white.
My father, who worked outside
for years, was the color
of weather. Just before I leaned
over to tell my mother
Dad wasn't gone after all,
I noticed his hands.

At first, I wasn't quite sure
if they belonged to my father
until I looked closer
and saw Dublin on his thumb.
I knew then there was no
mistake. All I could do
was kneel down next
to my mother, close my eyes
and listen to her cry.

The Way to Heaven

The woman who lives
in the apartment in back
of mine was born 80 years ago
in Paris, but is still French.
Every night she screams
at her cat until it becomes
the dog she always wanted
and barks.

I have nothing in common
with the 300 pound tenant
living next to me,
except for the wall we share.
He never goes to work
but goes on drunks
and falls into his wall
knocking pictures off mine.
The morning after my framed
map of the U.S. fell
to the floor, I read an editorial
on what bad shape the country
was in, although there was no
mention of how Florida
was not cracked in half.

Last week St. Paul's church
across the street caught fire.
Local news stations reported
a priest, who was writing a sermon

for Sunday Mass, started it
accidentally when he didn't notice
nearby curtains ignite with flames
from a paragraph on Hell.

I watched from my window
as smoke flowed out of a hole
in its roof, the way expensive
cigar smoke flows out of a big
man's mouth. Firemen fought
the blaze all night until the church
was no longer Catholic, then burned
Presbyterian for an hour before
they finally put it out.
On Sunday the parish went
to the new deli on 3rd
where they claim the chicken soup
works miracles.

Today I left the apartment
to buy a pack of cigarettes
I no longer smoke.
Sitting on the front steps,
a guy with long hair and beard
drinking a bottle of wine
said he was God, then pointed
to the church with his chin
saying the fire put him on
the street. As I walked away
he yelled, "You better start
fuckin' prayin' to me again
and while you're at it
bring me back some beer."

I bought a pack of Camels
at the newsstand, thought things
over for a moment, then headed
for the grocery store to get some
beer, just in case the way
to heaven is a couple of prayers
and a six-pack.

After Rain

Not far from where I'm sitting
on the beach, a log is lying on shore.
The ocean has been trying to set me
up with it for weeks but even in
this glare, I can see that months
rolling in surf has not quite made
it the woman I want.

I appreciate though what water
is trying to do for me and if the tide
weren't out, I'd thank it and
promise that when I'm ready
to be with someone again, I might
come back and learn to love wood.

I close my eyes and don't think
about the woman who once
loved me. Nor can I recall the first
night she invited me over for dinner,
lit candles, took out her jazz collection
and let Coltrane cook for us.
How easy it's been to forget the way
she made flowers flare or an arthritic
maple bud one more spring.

Coming to this island is teaching me
to accept whatever ends in life
is just another way to begin,

like it does in an arch of light
that hugs this bay after rain
and turns the beach so white, I'm
convinced all angels are sand.

from

Ready to Eat the Sky

(2004)

Turning Things Around

No matter how long a shower
I take, I still can't get this city
clean. I guess it doesn't matter
since I always knew I'd make it
to the top and now I have: 5th floor
of a five flight walk-up. It's a place
where I can shine like that guy
did in Math class back in high school.
For him it was grades, the right answers.
For me it's heat; with no AC I come up
with the right amount of sweat every
time. And I finally got the ringing
in my head to go away as soon
as I stopped paying the phone bill.
Within days I started getting in shape
after noticing how 1st Avenue with its heavy
traffic shed a few cars and is now
down to a single lane. So I started
running with it along the river too.
Have also been reading more but found
the quickest read was the face
of the woman on the 3rd floor
who always smiled as I walked
past her. She helped me quit
smoking when I found out nothing
could get me as high as her skirt.
And things keep getting better now
that I have a real identity. A couple
of months ago I wanted to know more

about my ancestors and started to trace
my family tree back to a maple in a park
across town then quit when I found
out I was Celtic. I discovered it
by accident during dessert last Friday night
when the cake I ordered kept crumbling
onto the plate like an Irish castle.

Taxi Ride

I hop into a cab
and when the driver says
where to, I check to see
which way the heavy traffic
is going then tell him
to follow it downtown.

He cuts through Central Park
the way I should have cut
through the crap that day
and didn't. I rest my head
against the seat that is as soft
as a woman's chest and think
for the first time in my life
I might be able to fall
in love with vinyl.

When I was a kid
I had an uncle whose round
face would light up
with a smile after a few drinks,
mess up my hair then give
me whatever change he had.
That's what the moon
looks like tonight, an uncle
working on another drink
and ready to put his hand
in his pocket to fork over
a couple of bucks.

Apartment lights gleaming
from high rises around the Park
are mixed in with stars
that slid down from the sky
during the heat wave last
week. Its hard to tell them
apart. At least I know in
this part of the city any star
I can reach by elevator
isn't worth the ride.

We come out on 58th Street.
Broadway glitters like a bracelet
filled with jewels and waiting
to be bought. I figure
it's a good idea to come back
for it later, then give it
to a woman who'll appreciate
how these lights sparkle
in all kinds of weather
and why traffic is the rarest
of gems whenever it dangles
from your wrist.

If You Want to Drive Rather than Walk the Rest of the Way Home

When you are on the road
under a sky you don't understand
every time it talks crow, stay with it
until you reach a dead cat lying
in the grass; his eyes are yellow
from the headlights on the car
that hit him. Rain has already
turned his fur rust, his belly
is still white from years of rubbing
against snow and every breeze
that passes through his open mouth
rips on teeth.

Across from him are two roads.
Take the one he didn't reach—
it's thin and gravel and sounds
like an old man clearing his throat
if your feet drag. It runs through
fields that were once Indian burial
grounds, so don't worry if a pickup
truck passes you with a ghost
of dust behind it, since the soil
it usually carries is haunted
with bone.

Where the road curves there's
a farm house the color of drought,
reminding you even here things
can go wrong and that you are right
so keep going. A quarter mile on
there's an orchard that looks apple
but is peach and then a potato
field that adds starch to the air
and if you're not careful a few
inches around your lungs.

You'll then come to a meadow
where blades of grass are dull
enough for cows to graze and never
cut themselves. Look for a horse
who wears a hat of flies in case
it rains, feed him an apple
you should have taken from
the orchard and he'll take you down
a small ravine to an old truck.
It lost its paint and tires
a few wars ago, but climb in
behind the wheel, start it up
with your throat, then sit back
and drive home, listening
to all those weeds in its engine purr.

Where You Want to Be

You wake early again
get out of bed, walk over
to the window and look down
at the street to see if anything
has changed and, of course,
it never does.

At first you think the blanket
in the vacant lot near
the corner is new until
a gust of wind blows it
into the air and shreds
it into a flock of pigeons.

And if all the new clubs
make sure the city never
sleeps uptown the way the papers
claim, then the people under
cardboard in the alleys and in
front of doorways down here
every morning is how it finds
a way to nap.

The steeple on St. Bart's a few
blocks away is a spike that nails
Christ into the sky if you can't find
anything on the street to believe in
but it does nothing for the bent
trash cans standing along the curb

like arthritic old men who know
the real purpose of any life is found
in what everyone else throws away.

A woman coming out of the grocery
store on the corner of 4th in a short
skirt and heels does a better
job stopping traffic than
the red light hanging from
a wire that would rather swing
like Count Basie in strong
wind than stop every car
it should.

When you hear the woman
you admit you love start
breakfast, cracking an egg
open like the dawn, its yolk
a perfect tiny sun, you
are convinced this is where
you want to be, walking towards
her, hungry and ready
to eat the sky.

Birthday

You hitch into the city
and walk a few blocks
until you find a small
hotel you can afford.
If you didn't have to leave
the next day, you'd offer
to paint it since you need
the work—tell the owner
to buy enough for two coats
but brush the second onto
yourself because it's getting cold
and there's only a sweater
in your suitcase.

The manager behind the desk
has a cigar stuck in the side
of his mouth like a cork,
his bald head shining—
waxed the way the floor
needs to be. When you can't
remember your name, you pick
another just as good, sign in
then ask him if he knows
when the first bus leaves
in the morning. He says forget it
since the cheapest ride in town
is the next woman he can send
up to your room in fifteen minutes.

You take the elevator
to the 4th floor, open the door
to 407, check out the bed,
chair and sink before flipping
on the switch. A bulb hanging
from a wire lights up
like an idea you're glad
even you never had.

Throwing your suitcase on
the bed, you walk over
to look out the window.
An apartment light two blocks over
goes on and lights the top
of a water tower shaped like a candle
on the warehouse across the street.
It reminds you today
is your birthday and when
a switch or wind blows
the apartment light out
you close your eyes and make
a wish.

A Few Extra Days

On the beach years of wind
have finished carving rock
into the face of a beautiful
woman who stares out to sea,
her eyes soft and peasant,
towards Spain or wherever
waves translate into Spanish.
I make sure to wear my watch
whenever I stroll by since
she never gives me the time
of day. Even so I can't help
complimenting her stone.

The sun is intelligent down
here, not just bright—it knows
how to keep people like me
content, showing why the blues
can only mean water and sky
and never a job I lost or the last
woman who walked away.

Along this stretch of beach
and beyond the point with the palm
tree that looks like Bob Marley,
sailboats are knives sharpening
their blades on wind and the one
a few yards off shore looks out
of shape with its spinnaker a large
belly that must be full of beer
rather than wind hanging over its bow.

I've decided to stay a few extra
days and go sailing by myself again.
Last night I left the harbor
at sunset, the sky the color
of a thin gold bracelet on the wrist
of a young girl. By midnight
I was lost until I used stars
lovers on land wouldn't need
to chart my way towards a bear
tamed by the moon then relaxed
and sailed towards the coast
under its paws.

Getting By

This old fishing village
is where the world turns
slowly on the blades
of a ceiling fan in a tavern
near the docks. I can
sit at the bar all day alone
and say nothing, dressed
in my favorite shirt
the loud one that's quiet
enough for me to listen as locals
still talk tuna and drink extra
beer to add pounds on
the stories of whatever
they once caught.

I heard that before schools
were private and Protestant
in the next county, they
were a few miles off shore and bass.
Fisherman caught more waves
than needed, gutted them
for the fish inside, then threw
back any whitecaps
they couldn't use.

Things changed when most
fish were caught
and those that stayed
decided to keep their mouths shut.

Then the village tried but couldn't
catch tourists who went
for the beach a town up the coast
used for bait.

Even though I never grew
up around water and the only
fishing I ever did was for compliments,
the day I drove onto Main Street,
I could see this village had learned
to do what I've always done—
to simply get by.

I saw it in the small shops
that were closed
and heavily salted with sea air
to keep them from spoiling in heat.

And later that night
how twilight over the harbor
was patched with stars
flags on boats lost in strong winds.
It was enough to make me stay.

Getting here is easy. Begin
with the last job you lose
or with a woman who believes
in you and says the moon
can be yours if you'll only reach for it.
Instead reach for another drink,
then sit back and do nothing

as the bourbon tells her that your old
car is big and yellow with a grill
grinning below a headlight
of eyes and is all the moon
you need.

The next day take 95 South
and keep driving until tired.
Turn on the local jazz station
and take the first exit between
Basie and Coltrane. Stay on that road.
It will pass through a piano
solo before leading into the village.

I'm beginning to think now
that I may never leave or even
bother looking for a real job.
What's the point when I know
every morning there will be a strong
breeze outside my window,
making leaves rustle like dollar
bills. It means I can afford
to stay in bed as long as I want,
since another day will come cheap.

Street Music

I'm on the street
where a guy once walked
up next to me and asked
for my wallet. I looked
at him then down
at the knife he was holding
and the point he was trying to make.
I was convinced and handed
it over. The year before
crime had come down
with the old tenements
and new buildings went up
faster than rents.
I watched him run across
town with what was left
of the old neighborhood
in his coat pocket.

The entire area is safer
now but more expensive.
The shops along Third
were torn down. Most
came back as French
or Italian boutiques, some
never came back or
were lost in the translation.
Across the street the tallest
building yet is under
construction; at the end

of the day workers come down
covered in white dust
from rubbing against clouds.
It's going up on the spot
where the magazine store
stood. Its owner ran it
for sixty years and had more
stories in him than
the high rise ever will.

Some things in the area
aren't what they seem.
Two years ago the section
of the river that runs
along the north side started
to jog and its banks
filled with concrete slabs
now closed on national holidays.
Although the traffic on First
is still heavy, cars keep changing.
What stays the same and never
changes is the music
found in women walking
in heels that are so high
you need an elevator
just to reach their ankles.
Listen and you'll hear
their hips sway back
and forth with the kind
of songs you'll swallow
and never want to hum.

Shadow Boxing

After his stroke
I wanted my father
the way he was:
picking up 50-foot ladders
as if they were toys
and putting them on
his green truck that was
a bit darker than Dublin.

I didn't want his arm
hanging limp at his side.
Instead I wanted him
crouching over, throwing
a right cross at air,
a jab on the chin of a breeze,
finishing up with a flurry
and a blur of fists.
Then see that smile one more
time as he said, not bad
for an old man of 65.

On Monday I visited his grave
and no matter how green
the grass is, it never looks
like him.

When I left I wanted my father
back again, even if it meant
that last month when words
were tools he couldn't find,
or sitting on the edge
of his bed waiting for my mother
to dress him—his shoulders
thin and drooping.

The Truth About Paris

Most of my relationships
last as long as a drag
on a cigarette. This time
I gave up on Christ
then Buddha but now
pray to Elvis since
he died for our songs.
And when a friend said
I have a big appetite
I told him he should see
how cancer eats.

In the bakery across
the street there are loaves
of bread lying in a pile
in the window like baseball
bats. Today I bought one
then headed to the park
to hit a few balls out
or get into a game.

By the time I got there
I had eaten most
of the loaf, until it fit
in my hand like a club.
So I took it home to make
a sandwich, knowing
this way I'll never get
to first base.

The truth is I like to travel.
Last month I met a woman
with a small birth mark
on her thigh that's shaped
like France. How easy it is
to go there now, if only
to touch Paris with my tongue.

Dogs

My brother and his wife
bought a hunting dog.
It's white with black patches.
There's one that's shaped
like Rhode Island, a small state
that isn't too heavy for a three
month old puppy to carry
around on his back.
As he gets older, stronger
and puts on weight, it will stretch
into Texas.

They have already taught
him to sit but he is still
too young to learn about Jesus,
so when they took him
to the beach, he tried walking
on water, fell in then turned
and attacked a wave,
ripping it to shreds.

A mound of cookie dough
on a plate is how he sleeps
on a round mattress and
dreams of rabbits or grouse.
For now a tennis ball
is enough to hunt down,
and sheets flying like ghosts

over rose bushes from
a neighbor's clothesline
is what makes him bark.

My brother and I take him
out on the lawn, throw
him a stick into tall grass.
He runs after it, his ears
that will never be trained
bounce and flap like a loose
shirt. He comes back
with the stick in his mouth
and every dog we ever
had as kids following him.
We can't believe how many
years have gone by since
we've seen them. Then we sit
down on the grass, smile
and watch all our dogs
running.

Apple Spider

My niece at age four
is already tired
of the language as we
know it. Instead
of orange juice she asked
for a glass of apple
spider and at lunch
at a diner in town
she wanted me to put
a quarter in the little
juice box next
to the table and play
a song.

When we got home
I walked up into her
bedroom in search
of some sort of proof
that she is what I always
suspected: a genius.
Perhaps there would be
books on linguistics,
philosophy, Shakespeare
or essays by Pound
who might have ignited
her passion to "make it new."

But there was nothing
by Plato under her purple
hippo, no critical works
amongst her coloring
books or Socrates hidden
behind her dolls. Later
when her mother claimed
her daughter can't even
read and the classics
for a four year old
are Barney and Lamb Chop,
I still wasn't convinced.

So when my niece
told me she heard
I liked poet trees,
then asked where do
they grow, we both
picked up our cold
glasses of root beard
held on to each other's
hand, then headed out
the door to see if any
were growing in
the backyard.

Grilled Fish

We had lunch
in a local trattoria
built into coastal rock,
picked a table on the deck
a few feet above water
that looked like the last
good novel I dove into.

A waiter came over
leaning on two metal canes.
He walked like stone
and his English was a coastline
of jagged rock. His smile
brought the sun closer,
suggested local specials,
and we said grazie
to things the sea didn't
need that day.

Another waiter brought
a pitcher of wine
with a round gold peach,
a tiny moon you can peel,
resting on the bottom.
We drank it with a salad
and tomatoes so sweet
and red the church should
make Satan blue.

Our main dish was grilled
fish that hadn't lost
their heads to the chef's knife,
or over the wrong women
the way I did a while back.
We didn't recognize them
either. They might have been
French, swam down here
for the day, then were tricked
by hook or net.

They tasted as rich
as the sun resting
on waves filled
with every gold coin
from every ship that sank
since Ceasar and kept
rolling towards shore.

Swimming

I'd like to attend
the schools these small
fish swim in to learn
how this water stays
so clear and if it's envy
of sky and rock that turns
it green. Lack of wind
or therapy must calm
waves and extra salt
helps me float.

On my back, I look up
at mountains holding
homes in their cliffs.
Some sit so high
at night with their lights
on, they mix with stars.
And if I were a local,
I would have known better
than to pick a kitchen
light to make a wish.

The current takes me out
even though there is no
sail on my chest, and where
I can see a twelfth century
tower that was built to warn
of Saracen invaders
who scared towns into

mountains, and when they
couldn't find God in churches,
killed priests instead.
Tourists are the only invaders
today along with tide
and boats from Capri.

By now I'm wet
enough to understand
the Tyrrhenian Sea must love
this coastline to be so warm
and maybe even me,
on my back, with the sun
on my lips, floating.

The Ride to Amalfi

The road to Amalfi
winds along cliffs
that are narrow as any
thought my uncle ever had.
I look out at the sky that goes
on and on like two locals
talking and see a fish flying
north towards Naples,
its scales gleaming in the sun.
When it is over a yacht
that could fit in my niece's
bathtub, it becomes a jet.

I close my eyes when
we come to a turn and try
not to look down over the ledge
where the drop is deeper
than the debt it took me years
to climb out of. The bus driver
tells us everyone who lives here
believes the rock up ahead
looks like the Madonna. I try
to think of a prayer with stone
in it, then a quick blessing,
with a pebble or two but can't
as it becomes just another
opportunity that passes me by.

On a ridge above us, there must
be enough soil for an orchard—
trees, two by two, in long lines
like young soldiers, fresh troops
still green behind the leaves
marching off to harvest, armed
with branches and lemons hanging
like grenades from their shoulders.
Then around the next turn
and at the bottom of the road,
the harbor and town open up
the way a man clearing his conscience
does, with the sun staring down
and listening like a priest who forgives
absolutely nothing.

The Last Saint

Even too much wine
can't stop all the hurt
you packed, but thought
Customs would never let
you bring into the country.
When they asked if you
had anything to declare,
you said the last ten years.

Somehow you can still
walk past the Medieval
tower that tonight is just
how the Amalfi coastline
gets a hard-on for water,
cars, moon or anything
that moves. So you sit
on a bench.

Low tide rubbing against
rock is how a song finds
a way out of your throat.
And to think you couldn't
speak a word of Italian
when the night began.
But since English never
made any sense and makes
even less now, you decide
never to speak it again.

A couple is standing in
front of you. The man looks
Polish enough to be the Pope
and the woman with him
is so large they must rub
her thighs down with olive oil
to squeeze her into Rome.
They are laughing but since
it's a joke you know the punch
line to, you laugh even louder.

Then they are gone and there
is a church like the one
in Sorrento where Christ
is stone. Before you think
about converting to concrete,
you are in an alley leaning
against a building older
than Octavian. A woman
is kneeling in front of you
opening your belt. And
this is where it happens,
the very moment when
you become the last saint
on the face of the earth
who doesn't have a prayer.

St. Andrew's Head

In the tenth century A.D.
St. Andrew preached
his way down the Southern
coast of Italy. Somewhere
between Sorrento and
Positano, he decided he must
leave something he valued
most to the Church when he
died. You might have thought:
a pouch of pepper, a few
drachmas, a favorite pair
of sandals repaired new
in Priano or even the goat
he converted by mistake,
when it was tied to a nearby
tree listening as he preached
to a group of Salerno pagans.
Instead St. Andrew decided
to leave the one true
and holy apostolic Church
his most prized possession—
his head. The same head
that now rests in a glass
box in the Dumo Cathedral
in the town of Amalfi.

The summer I visited
Amalfi, July was the hottest
on record before melting it.

Even the the Tyrrhenian Sea
looked more damp than wet.
Cafés surrounding the piazza
sold espresso dark
as midnight if you don't
pour in milk, stars or moon.
But I kept drinking water
from a woman's breast
who had been squirting it
from a fountain, and into
the mouths of locals and tourists
for centuries. Most
of the town goes back
to the Middle Ages, the sun
all the way back to Caesar.
I don't recall if the heat
caused the sun to slide down
the sky that looked more Spanish
than Italian or if a mountain
grew and covered it,
but by 4pm half of the piazza
was cut in shade darker
than wine, and cool enough
for me to head up
the Cathedral steps.

A few locals were sitting
on them. A large man,
who could sink Capri,
smoked a cigarette on
the first step. A few above
him an old woman, with a face

lined like a river after
it lost its water to drought,
ate a sandwich. A step
above her a young boy
pointed to my chest and
said, *American*. The sweat
stain on my shirt had formed
a map of the U.S.. I took
it off and kept my t-shirt on,
making it easier to climb
the rest of the steps with all
fifty states flung over
my shoulder. I headed
inside; just another tourist
there to look in the face
of a man whose had nothing
to hold onto for centuries,
the head of a saint in a glass box,
his eyes closed to the world.

While You Are Away

(for Celia)

I wanted to give you
something special tonight.
Perhaps dinner next
to the harbor where a warm
breeze comes in off
the ocean from Europe
and plucks the riggings
of sailboats along the docks
like Spanish guitars.
But it's winter, almost
midnight and you still
haven't arrived. You see
I've come to the realization
that everything that is broken
in me is yours. So I do
what I believe is right:
place two glasses on
the table near the window,
open a bottle of claret
and pour some into each,
then turn off the lights
wait and watch as the moon
floats in our wine.

Leaning Against August

Today the air is thick enough
for me to lean against
August and tie my shoe.
But no matter how hot this city
gets, I couldn't live anywhere else.
Even the garbage on the sidewalks
is really the only way to talk
trash and I can't deny anymore
there's something to the stain
a drunk pissed against
a building on 4th now that it
dried into a portrait of Christ.

Maybe I just go for how days
never dawn here—it's more
in the way they quietly show up.
Like the sun does when it looks
bloated and the color of beer
in this haze and hung over
2nd Avenue. Or any street that hums
with air conditioners resting
on windowsills like Polish
grandmothers looking down
at America when it was only
a few blocks long.

When my own AC broke down
I found it cheaper to play
my Miles Davis collection since

it cools off the entire apartment.
And I found it's a good idea
to keep extra change in my pockets
in case I see the blind man
who stands between 3rd and 4th
holding a paper cup with his dog
sleeping like a bagel at his feet.

He stands a block away
from where the woman
I've been seeing lives.
She's been unemployed for a year
but to keep busy she works
hard on our relationship.
I really care for her but until
I feel more, I keep stopping
in the little Italian joint across
the street from her place for a slice
of the pizza I love.

I guess the point is I can
adapt. I did to these buildings
the city rubbed against
so many times they turned dark.
Most are old tenements
no more than five stories
that I've read so many times
I can even quote you a couple
of floors by heart.

from

In the Eyes of A Dog

(2009)

Therapy

Once it was easier to love
an entire country rather than just
one person. Then you met a girl
who chewed gum that snapped
in her mouth like tiny firecrackers.
Each day you spent with her
was the Fourth of July and the first
night you slept together was the only
time in your life you felt patriotic.

You spend too much time thinking
about the past, though sometimes
it can't be helped. When the weather
report said the temperature would
reach the 60s over the next few days,
it made you take out your old Beatles
albums and play them all week.

Therapy is helping you deal more
and accept what's going on around you
now. So when you see another magazine
with a member of the Royal Family
on the cover and get disgusted with all
the money wasted on them, you have
to remind yourself how you always
wanted to be the next King of Swing.

You are also learning to make peace
with the fact that when the doorbell
rings the poodle in the apartment
next door will always bark in French
instead of English. And how the car horns
in heavy traffic along First in rush hour
are beginning to sound more and more
like Gershwin everyday.

The River

I sit on a bench next to the river.
The streets are far enough away
so by the time the sound of traffic
reaches me it massages my back.
I've come here before to figure
things out or just read. Last week
it was a novel I got hooked on,
inhaling every sentence as if they
were lines of coke. Mostly it's just
to look at the river; the tide stays wet,
each wave soaked all the way
through—making it easier for ships
to enter and leave the harbor.
When a page from a newspaper
grabs my ankle like a small dog
I pick it up, crumble it into
a basketball and shoot it into a trash
bin a few feet away as thousands cheer.

I then look across the river past
its banks that in this section of the city
are filled with rock and concrete instead
of cash, to the road and parked cars
where drivers go to come for twenty bucks.
I can almost make out a hooker's head
bobbing up and down in the front seat
as if it were floating on waves.

Dark water keeps most gulls away,
though eagles fly low in a flock
of tattoos on men who work tankers
and tugs. I know enough not to stare
at the water too long since it will pollute
my eyes and turn them brown but it's the only
river I've got. The pigeons that land near
my feet are always gray from rubbing
against sky and when I stomp my foot,
I know they'll fly away full on plans
that never worked out for me.
Plans that become just so many crumbs
I bring to feed them in brown paper bags.

Extra Income

Both sides of the street
are crowded with pedestrians
waiting for the lights to change.
An attractive woman across
the way stares in my direction,
so I inch closer to the curb
to get nearer to the heavy traffic
that always makes me look
thinner. A long line of cabs
creates a yellow spine, causing
First Avenue to look scared or
at least seem afraid to move uptown.

A jogger who pushes his way in front
of me should be wearing a t-shirt
to cover the hair on his back
that looks like smoke from hundreds
of tiny campfires his sweat
just put out.

Next to him an older woman
tells a friend she's on her way
to the beauty salon to have her hair
piled higher on her head since
she has been converting her curls
into apartments and renting them
out for extra income.

As the light changes and everyone
crosses I hear her say she didn't
need so much space, that's why
last month she moved downstairs
into the small studio nearest
her skull.

Shopping

An old man on the corner sells
white socks laid out on a table
like flounder in the Third Street
Fish Market. You pick out a size
nine, ask him to filet them so no bones
will get stuck in your feet.

You stop in the Army & Navy store
to buy a sweater, bright green,
but it's not as loud as the girl
in the apartment below yours
who screams God so often
when she fucks, you are beginning
to believe he really exists.

You stroll past the pawnshop
where a couple of months ago
you hocked ten years of your life
for one hundred bucks, ten more than you
expected. When you landed a job
you went back, saw them in the window
then went in and bought the guitar
they were next to instead.

On the next corner, the tall guy
from Ghana is back selling
watches from his briefcase.
You buy one every few weeks

after it breaks down but like the way
they run fast, making work days
go by so quickly Friday begins on Thursday.

Before going home you decide
to stop off and see the woman
you've been going out with
for the past month. You want
to apologize for last night's argument
but if she asks one more time
who you are trying to fool
you can hold up your wrist, point
to your Rolex and say, nobody but myself.

Sunday Afternoon, 1:15 PM

I've been watching Peter Gunn, an old TV show
cable has been running all week. He's a private detective
in the late fifties when cars had big fins
and traffic moved like a school of sharks.
The horn section from the theme music is so powerful
construction companies in the city should use it
instead of bulldozers to knock down buildings.

During a commercial, I look out the window
over the head of my father in front of an army
barrack. It's a photo where he is shirtless
with his right hand resting on a gun in a holster
hung low around his hips. He's in the Pacific
on a tiny island whose name I can never remember
but is so long its last four letters stretch past
the shoreline and rest in the surf. He's grinning,
young and happy to still be alive. He's the man
I didn't know—looking more action hero than father.

I have a good view of the East River.
A large tanker leaves the harbor and could knock
teeth out of the river's mouth if it isn't careful.
What's left of the August heat is bent, twisted
and piled on a barge a tug pulls past two new
high rises that are the size of a center and forward
the Knicks should draft if they want to make the playoffs.

I turn the TV off and decide to go out for a walk
noticing even with a clear sky the sun isn't shining.
It means the heavy weatherman on the local news
is standing in front of a map of the U.S.——his stomach
casting a shadow over the entire East Coast.
I still get ready knowing in a couple of moments the sun
will be out again as soon as he moves back towards the Midwest.

Poem with Mel Tormé's Voice

Rain has moved out of the city
and left behind fog that looks
like Mel Tormé's voice covering
the top floors of a high rise.
A woman leaning against an office
building takes out a cigarette, lights up
then keeps her mouth open to let the smoke
slowly crawl out. It travels up
past her eyes until her face resembles London.

Noise from traffic never stays
white as I walk between cars
to cross the street and avoid the guy
coming towards me. He lives down
the hall and feels he has to talk
although I always carry the conversation.
With a bad back, I thought it best
not to do any heavy lifting.

On Third I feel a shortness of breath
again. The doctor last week showed
me an x-ray of my lungs that looked
like two Porterhouse steaks. He said
they were fine and it was nothing more
than nerves. It's just that I worry
he might be wrong. In a few minutes,
I feel fine again and with the sky clearing,
I make my way home.

I take the elevator to the roof, pleased
it's an express, stand there and look out
at the East River. I have a good view
of Queens, its lights are low
and glowing—charcoal perfect for grilling.
So I hurry down to my apartment,
come back with a can of beer,
pull the pin like it's a grenade,
throw a couple of burgers on Astoria
and listen to them sizzle.

Eating a Herd of Reindeer

My wife is in the kitchen making
holiday cookies she will place in tins
and send to family and friends.
I walk in to find her humming as she
mixes eggs, sugar and vanilla in a bowl
with a wooden spoon like the one my mother
chased me and my brothers with as kids.

I watch her fill the press with dough
thick as clay then rest the front down
against a pan and click the trigger
until there are enough wreaths to hang
on every door in the apartment building.
On top of the oven a tray of stars cools,
an entire galaxy covered in white icing.

She shifts powdered sugar over another
batch on the counter, it falls over them
like a light dusting of snow that covers
everything but the street. And I enjoy
watching her—maybe it has to do
with the way she measures everything
exactly, or how I can always find
a smudge of flour on her neck and forehead.

The world I knew is the one I bolted
the door against every night when I got home.
But this is something I didn't expect, a world
that is as warm as a favorite old sweater

with holes in its elbows. And I can simply
walk into it, open a tin of reindeer cookies,
bite off an antler or two, sit down at the table,
eat a few more, then pour a large glass
of milk to help wash down the entire herd.

Butterfly

A casting director called—
told my wife, Celia, to come down
to the studio to meet him.
She was thrilled. It's an afternoon
soap that I've never watched.
I did know the woman who plays
the lead role since she is more famous
for all the Emmys she never won.
When she did win on her twentieth try,
she made the covers of all the papers;
a thin, pretty woman, who looked as flat
as Iowa holding the statue in both hands.
It was a little guy with gold wings
holding up the world, a kind of globe
with holes in it. The kind I've learned
how to live in. It reminded me
of a wiffle ball that I wanted to take outside
to hit with a bat, just to see how it feels
to knock the world around for a change.
Then my mind raced: he offers Celia
a role. In a month her fan mail piles up.
The network has no choice but to change
the title from: *All My Children* to *All My Celia*.
After her first year, her first Emmy.
She makes the covers of all the magazines,
smiling, holding it in her hand and me next to her
in a tux I bought with a bow tie resting
like a butterfly at my throat.

An Act of Seduction in the Twenty-First Century

You know as well as I
there is nothing more
than a piano between us.

So please rest your head
gently against my hip before
the moon burns a hole in my pocket.

If you close your eyes
perhaps you will see what I
did this morning at breakfast.

When I poured maple syrup
over a piece of French toast
it settled into a portrait of Christ.

Before I go any further you should
know this about me: I am
the kind of man who does not

believe in much of anything.
Now you will not be surprised
when I tell you what happened

next. I cut into it with my fork
and ate, just to feel what it is like
to chew on redemption.

A Type of Love Story

You gave up on most things
over the years until you met
a woman whose legs just wouldn't quit.
And when she slid into a pair of heels
her calves flared ever so slightly
as if to say: get down on your knees
and if you have a tongue in that mouth
of yours take it out and lick
until you are convinced this is the only
way home. And that's exactly what happened.
You got down on your knees and licked
all the words you would never use onto
her legs, a type of love story only you
would ever want to read again.

Smoke

The guy who lives upstairs
and has never spoken to me
stops to say his mother died
last week. His eyes are wet.
He had her cremated but didn't know
where to spread her ashes since
there were a few places she loved.
He doesn't listen when I whisper
sorry. In Maine he sprinkled
just her right hand on a mountain
along with some toes, an elbow,
a bit of ear. The rest he spread over
a beach in Rhode Island until
he got down to her smile that he decided
to keep in an urn in his apartment.

I didn't want to hear anymore
about death or think about cremation.
Sorry I say to him again and that I
have to get going. On the way to the train,
I think it over, decide I will be cremated
someday too, and now would be a good time
to practice so it might not be such a shock
when the first flames reach my toes.
That night I light up an expensive cigar
to see how life can burn slowly and how my ashes
look in a tray or at least why they are worth
the smoke it takes to get there.

Traffic in Your Chest

Last week the sound
of a passing siren got stuck
in your throat, turned it red
and sore. Then you worried
hearing traffic in your chest
every time you coughed.
It hurt so badly, you went
to the doctor who prescribed
antibiotics that cleared it up
along with the congestion
on Fourth Street.

You are much better now—
even enjoyed the way the first
snow dusted the grass in the park,
like sugar, making it look
so sweet you had to stop
in the diner across the way to order
a cup of coffee and a slice of lawn.

Walking home you almost bought
the newspaper at a stand on Fifth
until you saw the headline and lead
article about another killing
on the West Side. Even though you've
changed, it still made you
feel ashamed remembering how
for years you kept killing time
whenever you got the chance.

As you head uptown you pass
an old girlfriend's apartment building
and recall that last argument,
the one where she yelled you need
to be more open minded, flexible
and should learn to bend more.
So when change fell out of your pocket
onto the sidewalk, you wished
she had been there to watch you
bend all the way over to pick it up.
It was worth the fifty cents
just to prove her wrong.

Mango

(St. Maarten)

As soon as I walk into
the hotel room I throw my
suitcase on the bed and walk
out to the deck to get a better
look at the ocean. Palm trees
begin to applaud, turning my face
red before the sun reaches it.
I don't know what to say
since I packed some Spanish
in with my shirts but forgot
to bring any French, so I just smile
in English and hope it will translate.

I peer over their heads at the Caribbean
and watch a surfer who looks strong
as the dollar. Another is pulled
by a parasail—a big red belly filled
with wind showing how the air has put
on some extra weight but is still
powerful and in shape. Waves crashing
along the shore break up voices
except for a nearby child's who yells
to her mother she wants a peanut butter
and jelly fish sandwich.

And I can see an island named Dog
dozing like a rock in the sun. It doesn't
stir even with gulls walking on its tail
or get up and chase a jet ski that just
passed by it. To its left, waves break
against each other forming a long white
ribbon young girls cut into strips to tie
their hair back.

A few feet away a couple of locals sit
at an open bar drinking and talking
fish. Their voices roll up and down
sounding like the Caribbean after years
of it drying in their throats. They are telling
stories of sharks they have seen or that attacked
them. I would like to join in, buy a round
and try to fit in with stories of my own
about lawyers who attacked me. For now
I'm just glad to be here for another week,
the sun already setting and the color of mango.

In the Eyes of a Dog

I am having a drink in an open bar
on a beach in St. Maarten's. On the radio
Piaf is singing another Greek song,
since I don't speak a word of French.
The waitress who walks on waves
is singing with her, smiles the way
the sky does here, and places another
drink in front of me.

Over at the bar an Englishman complains
loudly how London isn't what it once was
and has changed. I want to tell him of course
it has, Dickens is dead and Churchill
is a cigar. When he gets even louder and says
something about fags to the guy mixing drinks,
I almost throw my glass at him then remember
he is only asking for cigarettes.

When I left home a close friend was still
feeling low after his wife walked out
on him six months earlier. That's why
everything on the island is so expensive.
The dollar is low too—it's just another
guy whose wife walked out a few months
ago. At least the chips are complimentary
along with the breeze coming in off the ocean.

A dog that has been roaming around
the bar stops next to my chair and stares
at me. The look in his eyes is familiar.
It's the kind of look that says I'm lost
and don't understand where I am but since
I'm standing here doesn't mean I want your scraps,
it means I made it through the day, but if
you have an easier way to get through another
I'll take it.

If the waitress didn't chase him away,
I would have told him this is how
you can at least get through another hour:
that the rocks the drinks are poured over will melt,
nothing can be built on them. So if you walk
the wooden planks on the floor to where
the sand begins and is stained white with stars,
the beach means more whenever it becomes
a piece of sky to walk home on.

Kissing the Sky

The surf along the beach
sounds like jets leaving
a runway. Surfers fly
on waves that break into
the color of cream I pour
in coffee, to make it look
as tan as my skin.

The tall men with dreadlocks,
swaying to music on the bluffs,
are palm trees and seals
sliding in on smaller more slippery
waves, become swimmers
in wet suits when they reach
the shore then get up to walk.

Salt on every breeze coming
in off the ocean is more
than I sprinkle on steak,
and the wind must have traveled
all the way from Europe,
since every gust looks French.

Here the sand is so white
the next angel I see will look
gray. And the sun setting over
the horizon is how my mother

sits on a couch, her gold dress
spreading over its cushions,
at a party that never ends
in a photo on my desk.

She said she always wanted
to move to the coast. So just
in case it is her, I pack up
my things, climb the tallest
bluff, lean my head back,
close my eyes and kiss the sky.

The Cavendish Firehouse Benefit Dance

After dinner we drove home
on the road that goes over
a mountain's foot and next
to a stream that runs even
at night. Insects hit the headlights
like snow flurries would if
August had more December in it.

We talked again about how much
we enjoyed dinner and agreed
the fish was so good it must
have loved water. She turned on
the radio to classical music,
promising to teach me more about it.
Somewhere in the middle of Bach
and Mozart was a lake she pointed
to where each winter the ice grows
thick and deep as trout. It was
the one she and her sister drove
their jeep on last January, parked
over perch and went skating.

I almost hit a dog that ran
in front of the car, but couldn't stop
the clock on the dashboard
from hitting midnight as we entered
Cavendish. We noticed a bright
light glowing from the center of town,
as if the moon had crashed,

then heard music, followed
a line of pickup trucks parked
along the street to a banner, announcing:
The Cavendish Firehouse Benefit Dance.
It hung over a wide driveway in front
of the firehouse, with a local band
and people dancing. We both
wanted to stop for a few moments
to check things out.

An old lady who looked more
like New Hampshire than Vermont,
sat next to a five dollar donation box
and a table covered with homemade
desserts. She said the dance
and any food sold helped pay
for repairs on the firehouse. The new
wing looked to me like it was built
with concrete but she claimed
it was built with cake. We bought
coffees the color of the brownies
we decided looked so rich we couldn't
afford them, then went to sit
on a small hill next to the blacktop
to watch people dance. I held
her cup while she sat down.
Flowers grew wherever
her print dress spread over grass.

Everyone dancing were locals—
farmers dressed in jeans,
baseball caps and t-shirts with the names
of trucks and machines on them.
A large man managed a smooth
two-step with a tractor on his chest.
And we smiled at a woman who kept
spinning until she drilled a hole
in the blacktop and couldn't move.
The band took a break after a song
about a cowboy who could never
love his wife the way he loved
his horse. She then looked at her watch,
saying it was already 1:30 AM
and we should really get going
since Weston was still forty minutes away.

The night had cooled as we strolled
back to the car and trees began rustling
their leaves with a tune that sounded so green
I knew that even I could dance to it.

Camden

For centuries ocean bit into
this coastline, rocks dripping
from its surf along the shore
before it left on every tide. In
town lobsters are on plates
and shirts; tourists walk on fish.
Boats leave postcards to cast
their nets, drop pots and some
carry the r's locals never use
when they talk and dump them
two miles out. In the leather shop
bags hanging on walls are faces
of fisherman sleeping on boats
anchored on canvas in the gallery
windows along Main Street.
In the park a Union soldier rests
on his musket looking tired as granite
with the harbor and all his wars
behind him. On the hill the Methodist
church wears a steeple on its clock
like a wizard's hat. Every hour
its bells ring hosannas into the wings
of gulls and rattle bowls of chowder
until the next faithless man can at least
believe in cod. And at night when mist
covers the moon it's just another porch
light kept on behind a screen so whenever
you leave home you can always find
your way back again.

Hiking

My brother and I take a gondola
up the side of the mountain.
When the wind makes it rattle,
I feel more uneasy than Italian.
At 7000 feet we hike the rest
of the way, then take a break
when the air becomes thin as
Audrey Hepburn but with a view
more beautiful.

At the bottom of a ravine,
we notice a small lake that reflects
everything moving above it.
From where we stand it looks
like a piece of sky that fell
during last night's storm.
When an elk walks out of a clump
of trees, with antlers we could hang
our clothes on, he goes over to the water's
edge and drinks down a cloud.

The dark peaks of a mountain,
in back of a ranch with a large
herd of ants or cattle, look
like icing on top of a cake,
when baked with rock, tree and snow.
And Main Street in Steamboat Springs
is the length of a 12-inch ruler

a nun used in math class to smack
our hands when things didn't add
up the way they should. Since
then I found most things never do.

To our south another storm
with a dark curtain of rain
hangs down on a town whose
buildings and farms are as big
as the periods I used on the postcards
I sent home. It won't reach us
for another hour, enough time to
get back.

We decide to take another path
down, with the rest of the valley
stretched out before us, a green
rug our mother would never
have let us walk on with our shoes.

Baja

On the map the Baja Peninsula
looks like a horse's leg; you are
renting a small apartment near
the hoof in San Jose. There's a mountain
in the window whose peak is shaped
like the Parthenon overlooking the Sea
of Cortez that sits in for the Aegean.
Large waves keep rolling in; they seem
furious at the beaches for making
them end in surf, so they crash
and spit foam. You have never seen
anger like this before, the kind
where there is so much wet behind it.

The men here stare, whistle and hit
on every woman who looks or may be
a tourist. Even the stars wink at
the coastline that has real curves
or must look full figured from the sky.
And there are thousands of stars.
Every evening you can find the Big
Dipper hanging over your head.

In Old Town you notice a small
kidney shaped pool in back
of a house that was boarded up. You
regret no longer speaking to a friend
at home who is on dialysis, needs
a transplant and is waiting

for a donor. You almost call
to tell him about it then decide
not to since he'd only yell
his illness is none of your business
anymore and besides the chlorine
has to be a perfect match.

You have already fallen into
a routine here. Every morning
you get coffee going, roll eggs
in a flour tortilla the way you
never could roll a joint. The days
are long with an hour or two
left over you just don't need, so
you trim, filet and feed them
to the skinny mutt who followed
you home and never left. And
you have decided to stay longer
than planned since the sun is just
the way you like it: hot and not too
spicy.

Capri

We take the ferry to Capri
from the dock at Positano.
There isn't a cloud in the sky,
that is clear as English, as we
head up the Amalfi Coast.
The mountains remind me
of my father napping after
a large dinner. I can make
out cars shining in the glare
as they move along the cliff
road that is thin as pasta
and for the first time ever
a bus becomes a gleam in my eye.

Twenty minutes later we can
spot Sorrento that is now
a porcelain dish shattered against
stone and as the waves rock and roll
like Elvis; a seasick young
woman the size of a small village
outside Salerno is helped down
from the top deck. I know little
Italian but the look on her face
is easy to translate. It takes
four crew members to help her
on the steps and over to the railing.
And then there is Capri: rising up
out of the water along with something
else to shake my beliefs. Perhaps

there is a God—who else could
have dropped those rocks into
the Sea of Naples just for the hell of it.

The ferry pulls into Marina Grande.
It's filled with shops, cafes,
tourists and boats with names
like the dinners on the menu
in the little Italian joint back home
on 1st. We stop in the Café Augusto
for a cup of espresso with a smile
of lemon floating in it, pay
with Monopoly money then decide
to take an open-roofed bathtub taxi
since we only have a few hours
until the next ferry. We follow
a road up a hill that is long
as a novel to the Villa Jovis
where Tiberius held court,
and where goats have ruled since
45 A.D. and then to the Salto
di Tiberio, a cliff, where he pitched
villagers into the sea since
soccer wouldn't be invented
for another thousand years.

We meet a local who speaks
to us in broken English—most
words fall out of his mouth
in pieces that could never be
glued back together. He tells us
we need a wick not just a day

to see Capri, how he loves basketabowl,
The New Yucka Nooks and that once
he spent two wicks in the downatone
zone of Manhattana. He shows
us a short cut to take on foot,
rather than take a cab, since we
can see more that way.

We follow his route, stop
in the Gardens of Augustus
just to let our eyes fill with cliffs,
sky and water. Waves roll
like the r's in the mouths of two
old men arguing over wine
outside a café along the Via Camerelle.
The water looks green, young
but gives away its real age
when it reaches the shore, exposing
its white beard of surf. So we
decide to hurry down and catch
the next ferry before the Sea of Naples
becomes too old to carry one more
boat back to Positano.

from

The Unemployed Man
Who Became A Tree

(2011)

Insomnia

You can never see the moon
that should be hanging over
Fourth Street and since you know
all about compromise you settle
for yellow circles from traffic
lights that slide across
the bedroom wall.

Most nights are like this—
not being able to sleep.
If you doze it's usually too
late to dream so you sweat
and don't even bother to turn
on the fan since like everything
else lately, it only blows.

When the walls begin to talk
or mumble it's usually a TV
in the next apartment and
for some reason you are back
in your parents' living room
watching their old black and white
RCA, everyone on the screen
the color of priests and nuns.

Your mother is on the couch,
her belly big as a basketball
filled with your sister. And now
your sister with kids

of her own and a son who
is already the age of a good
bottle of scotch. You love him,
he loves the Knicks, but what matters
most is his sweet outside shot.

All the women you ever dated
must have gotten together
and taken the early morning express
bus into the city. There's no other
way to explain the chill
in the breeze that just came
through the window.

And when you hear a cop car
hit some potholes then watch
its red light, the color of the sore
throat you just got rid of, speed
across the ceiling, it makes you
realize how lonely you are.
As the siren fades you almost
wish it would come back, loud
enough this time so you could turn over
on your side, put your arm
around it and fall asleep.

Milk

On a warm night in upstate
New York during the summer
of 1948, Charlie Parker got out
of a brand new Pontiac, the bass
player from his quintet was behind
the wheel. Clubs along 57th Street
were an hour behind them. Parker
had grabbed the case with his sax
in it from the back seat and walked
out onto a field. He was off drugs,
clean for at least six months
but knew he'd never be clean
as the air he breathed.

A herd of cows watched him walk
in front of them, place the case
on the grass, open it and take out
a bent piece of sky the color of dawn.
Then he blew on it as his fingers
like a flock of small dark birds flew
up and down. The cows listened, stopped
chewing but couldn't prevent their tails
from swinging like the Basie rhythm
section. Sounds they never heard
came out of a hole in the sky.
Then it stopped. He placed it back
in the box and walked away. Within
hours the green grass they began
chewing again turned the milk in
their bellies white.

Looking for Work

I'd been out of work for a month
and knew it was time to get going
on my job search. So I got out
of bed, gazed out the window, looked
for a job, saw nothing that interested
me, crawled under the covers again
and fell back to sleep.

An hour later, I got up, brewed
coffee, made it strong, the color
of wet road, then traveled a mile
with my throat until the pot was empty.

I didn't go out at all the day
before but knew everything worth
missing was just outside my door
in the paper. Even with Monday
folded over with a crease through
noon, a dollar seemed too
expensive for a day I basically
slept through.

The lead story reported a man
was shot just a few blocks
away, and though I hate guns,
I rifled through the rest of the paper,
tossed it on the floor then went
over to the refrigerator, even though
I don't believe in miracles, and opened

it. None was going to take place on
that day either: no food appeared
just an old piece of steak I cooked once,
that looked raw as last December.

With the temperature reaching
for 90° again and knowing
it shouldn't reach for anything
beyond its grasp, I decided to get
dressed and walk over to St. James.
It's a Catholic church but since
the saints inside are still concrete,
I like to go in on weekdays where
it's cool, dark and empty. The strange
part is it feels like home. I've decided
it's the candles who look like my
relatives. Irish. Each flame a jig,
lit up on Guinness instead of matches.

The Corner

I stand on the corner
in the middle of a heat wave,
dressed in a white linen shirt
and pants with creases so sharp
I cut my finger putting them on.
It has been in the 90s all week
but it's clear to anyone who looks
my way where the coolest spot
in the city is today.

A red '56 Buick slides by
with the kind of curves
a man can only fantasize about
and makes any woman who looks
turn green. When a friend
of my father's walks by, stops
to say she heard he died
and was sorry for my loss,
there was no way to tell
her it was a profit, or running
every day for a month and
dropping ten pounds was the real loss.

After she left, my brother
who lives around the block
walks by. We pretend
not to see each other since
we haven't spoken in over
a year. Even if I add a few

extra miles jogging, I'll never
be able to cover the distance
between us.

As I look over my shoulder
to see if he is gone, I catch
my reflection in the window
of the store I'm standing
in front of. Lights from the sign
above it and from the deli
next door melt across my face,
making me look like a Sioux
warrior on my way to Custer.
I like the look, then take
a cigar from my pocket, and
light it on the next hot breeze
that passes by, just to make sure
another hour will go up in smoke.

Promises

I'm standing at the corner
of Seventy-Second and York.
My niece who is eight and already
beautiful holds my hand. I warn
her again not to trust lights or cars
that fly by like summer.
She looks up and tells me not
to worry. She knows. But how
could she know I already worry
about the first guy who falls
in love with her. The kind of guy
who promises her the world, when
he can't even deliver Brooklyn.
Or the first guy she falls for, the one
who at night wants to take the lights
from buildings along Park and tie
them into a bracelet around her wrist
then slides the brightest light
from a penthouse on to her finger.
Before I can lean over to tell her
that the sparkle will go out as soon
as the sun comes up, she
points to the walk sign and says
we can go. Instead I remind her
to make sure the traffic light is red
and strong enough to stop
all the cars it should. As we
cross a woman passes us
with a dog the color of smog.

My niece asks if I can get her
a puppy just like it. She's not allowed
to have pets yet but I find myself
promising to buy her a dog
that's even bigger, smarter
and with extra fur,
if she wants.

The Distance Between Fog and Times Square

After I moved into my first
apartment, every time the phone
rang I expected it to be
the voice of a woman sounding
like slow approaching fog
or a thousand Playboy
magazines. For months
I slept alone under an old
skylight on the top floor
of a five flight walk up.
Every time it stormed
raindrops hitting the glass
sounded like a typewriter
working on another story
until there was a sixth floor.
I soon learned what was real
in the city and what was fake.
The ten-inch statue in a shop
window along Times Square
could never be the Statue of Liberty
but did turn out to be the next woman
holding up her arm to hail a cab.

Walking Across America

Our third grade teacher
was a Dominican nun
who dressed in white robes.
Sister was short and thick
and when she stood still
to begin each day with a prayer
she looked like vanilla ice cream,
three scoops piled on top of each
other. Her black veil, chocolate
syrup pouring over her head
and down her back. I closed
my eyes and prayed for dessert.

The classroom was decorated
with letters of the alphabet, some
that for the last three years hadn't
made much sense. The C was an O
with its right side missing,
W was an M that fell on its head
and Z proved Zorro was still alive.

Math made even less sense—
the day three times two equaled
eight, the thick piece of plywood
that slammed against my back
was the palm of Sister's open hand.
And when she stood next to my desk
and shouted again, I closed

my eyes and braced myself. Six
was the lucky number that made
her move onto the kid at the desk
in front of mine.

During geography she told the class
to take out our large maps
of the US and spread them
across our desks. After I got
my pencil out, I noticed a tiny
roach standing on Maine.
It headed down along the East coast,
couldn't find Florida hanging over
the edge then headed west before
resting in Texas.

I kept watching as it made
its way to California and didn't
notice Sister walk by or her fist
shaped like a sledgehammer
come down and smash it all over
San Diego. She didn't even stop—
just kept walking up the aisle slowly,
the long rosary that hung on
to her belt rattling at her side.

On Cold Days Like This

I hear a cape flapping over
my head, convinced this time
it's Superman. When I look up
to greet him, it turns out to be
the flag over the doors of the Second
Avenue Post Office. The wind
is so strong I notice it lost a star
and wonder if maybe Utah is now
floating over New Jersey.

The traffic is heavy as cheesecake
and sounds like the Basie horn
section tuning up before a gig.
A guy walks over with a cigarette
in his mouth and asks if I got
a light. As I search my pockets
I notice his boots and cowboy
hat and figure he must be from
the West Side. I can't find any—
consider the torch I'd been carrying
around for my ex but remember I put
it out a few days ago, tell him sorry.

And she was the same woman
who told me if we ever broke up
I'd be lost without her. Before
I got involved again, I made sure
to know every section of the city
until I knew it like the back

of my hand or when most of Second
Avenue ran down my index finger
towards my wrist. On cold days
like this, I can warm up my hands
and at least thirty blocks by simply
putting on my gloves.

The Week the Factory and Pancreas Closed Down

You were no more than eleven
waiting in the car in the A&P
parking lot while your mother
shopped and had to pee so badly
you got out and stood in front
of your dad's new Buick, leaned
up against it so no one could see,
opened your fly and started pissing.
You remember how you couldn't stop,
water draining out of you until
there was nothing left but sand
in your mouth and your eyes went
dry. You finally stopped when the grill
shaped like a smile frowned and all
you wanted to do was lie down like a lawn
and sleep. The factory right across
the street acted like your pancreas,
and went on strike the same week—one
stopped turning out ball bearings,
the other insulin. You considered
yourself luckier only ending up
with a loss of weight, a pitchfork of ribs
and diabetes—the factory with a loss
of jobs, boarded windows and rats.

Travel

I admit I see things a bit differently.
At the corner when the Don't Walk sign
lights up, its red hand stopping everyone
from crossing the street, I think it's an old
friend, so I wave, walk over to say hello
and almost get hit by a truck. And when
there is a sudden downpour, and everyone
starts to run trying not to get soaked, I
just tilt to the left, stroll between raindrops,
and stay perfectly dry. Then I stopped
looking at myself in storefront windows,
when I began to develop a crush, I'm
embarrassed to admit, on my reflection.

At least I knew enough to end things before
they went any further. For the past three
months though, I've been dating a woman
my friends make fun of whenever they see
us together. It's true she towers over me,
but I can't hear what they have to say since
I've never learned how to listen to anyone.
Besides, they never would understand how
I love to travel and at six feet, three inches
in heels, she is worth the trip.

The Unemployed Man Who Became a Tree

I lost my last job in July
then spent the rest of the summer
working on a tan. With little money
left, I searched the want ads
until coming across an opening
for a tree. The spot was just a few blocks
away near the path that runs along
the river. I hurried over to the square
patch of dirt in the concrete where
the city cut the last tree down.
Then stood on it, looked around,
liked the area and decided to take
the position. Within minutes my legs
went stiff as my feet began to root
the soil. My arms branched out,
skin became bark. The paper didn't
say what kind of tree was needed
although my limbs looked maple,
from the waist down, I was all oak.

By evening I was just about done
and even began thinking like wood:
how to bud April green enough
to get spring going early this year.
The only bird I ever cared about
was Charlie Parker, now I wanted
a flock to rest on my limbs,
build a nest on the highest branch
that sprouted from my ear—

a place to call home and a place safe
from cats. By evening the fog that crawled
in on its knees was gone and there I was,
alone, holding up the moon in my branch
shaped like a right hand for the entire
city to see—smiling.

Antigua

You are having a drink
in Redcliffe Quay.
Driving here you passed
goats that roam freely
on the island and noticed
one whose face looked like
Uncle Sam's under a tree
with palms shooting out
of its top like fireworks
on the Fourth of July. They
made you feel homesick
for the first time in weeks
and one more drink may help
you forget why you left.

At a table near you someone
is speaking German. Two
women speaking French
have drinks the color of sunset
and sip the sky through straws—
two guys at the bar are laughing
so loud anyone can translate it.
No one speaks English and if
you are honest with yourself,
you never really spoke it either.

The night sky here is warm
and black with a wide
smile and glittering jewels,
looking like the waitress
who brings you another local
drink with rum and a way
to go home. You decide to take
these languages, blend them
together into one, name it
after the next cool breeze, then
learn to speak it fluently.
When you are back in the States
and are rejected again and again
since no one understands
a word you are saying, at least
you will finally have the only
worthwhile reason for not ever
getting what you want.

It's About Time

—for Maureen

Drinking coffee with my sister
in her kitchen, I give in and agree
being the only girl and the youngest
with three older brothers couldn't
have been easy. Try awful she adds
before taking another sip from her cup.
I knew my brothers and I teased her
so much she often cried but tried
to convince her we stopped when her
skin turned pink. And yes we did pinch
her on occasion, she was too cute not to.
The way she remembers, it was more
like every day. At least the hardest pinch
she still feels on her cheek came from
our oldest brother. That's why no one talks
to him anymore, I offer with a smile.
She just frowns, knows what I really mean
and asks if I want a refill.

As she pours more coffee into our cups,
I notice it has begun to flurry. It reminds
us again about how in our house as kids
snow was a four-letter word. It crippled
our dad's roofing company, his men couldn't
work and cost him a lot of money, he'd complain.
When school closed every storm and put
our dad in a bad mood, we couldn't show

how thrilled we were for the day off until
we went outside and played in drifts.
In summer we made sure to bring home
ice pops but never snow cones.

After our parents died, my sister made sure
my brothers and I who were still single
were invited to her house for dinners since we all
belonged together she told us. She was such
a great cook we always showed up often
at dinner time, on all major holidays,
then on holidays she never heard of.
After her son was born, I heard her say
on the phone she had one child, then looked
over at us finishing dessert and said,
but I have a lot of mouths to feed.
We both watch the snow falling and begin
to pile up like the pages in a new short
story she is working on. She complains about
not having enough time to write and asks
when will I finally write a poem about her.
I know she is only half kidding, though
she doesn't know this one is for her. So
I add the last two lines, leave out the stanza
about how lucky we are to be this close
for another poem, then slide it across
the table and ask her to read it. She puts on
her new glasses, that of course make her
look thinner, reads it, slowly takes them off
and says it's about time.

Santorini

I didn't know how high up
on the caldera our villa
was until I stood on the terrace
and looked down at a toy boat
a child lost, before realizing it was
a cruise ship and the yacht sailing
past Skaros, I could pick up
and put in my pocket along
with the rest of the Euro coins
I'd been carrying around since Athens.
And where the sun reached
the surface of the Aegean, candles
were flickering inside waves.

A woman standing on a rock
was the size of a matchstick
I thought about using to light
my cigar until I found my own,
lit up, then let smoke the size
of a cloud float out of my mouth,
since there was no rain in it
to spoil the day. And I've learned
the man yelling next door
is how Greeks whisper.

Tiny white churches no bigger
than doves are scattered all over
the island. A flock sits along
the cliffs leading towards the town

of Oia on the northern tip
of the caldera that from here looks
like vanilla icing melting over
a slice of rock.

I pull up a chair, sit down and
stare deeply into this view the way
I never could into the eyes of a woman
until they belonged to my wife,
let my skin turn the color
of iced tea, then noticed how there
were now white caps on the water,
or thousands of angels swimming
towards shore.

Santorini at Night

I sit on the terrace under
a moon that will stay Greek
until I leave. The sky is clear
and the air cool as Steve McQueen.
I can see Oia, a town on the northern tip
of the caldera, its lights glowing
like hot coals just perfect
for grilling steaks on. To the south,
the lighthouse on Akrotiri keeps
winking at me. I'm flattered
knowing the most beautiful
coastline I've ever seen
is hitting on me, but I can't
imagine acting on it or taking
the leap and dropping four
thousand feet—the only way to fall
in love with this view. And
there is the Big Dipper sparkling
like it belongs in my mother's
kitchen. A cruise ship moving
as slow as a Russian novel passes
under it and in front of an island
a volcano left for taking Atlantis.
It looks like a dog sleeping.
When I leave I plan to whistle
until it wakes, gets up, shakes
its rock into fur and follows me
all the way to the airport with its
tail wagging.

Athens

(Plaka)

We stop at a taverna in Plaka
and pick a table outside where we
can have drinks and watch tourists.
The Acropolis rises up over the city
and in back of your wife's chair
who looks elegant wearing the Parthenon
as a crown. Ancient architects built
these narrow streets for citizens to walk,
horses, carts and maybe motor scooters
that to this day zigzag through the crowds.
Shop owners try to flatter then hustle
tourists into their shops. If anyone
looks German, Berlin is the best, if
Italian, long live the Pope and when
you walk by, the Bronx is beautiful.

At the table next to you a woman
speaks good English but sneezes in French.
At another, a Belgian couple is telling
jokes, getting drunk and laughing too loud.
When one comes over with his camera
and motions for you to take a picture,
it's a chance for you to get rid of them
with one shot. You take your time,
aim and shoot but miss by a mile.
As the tables fill around you everyone
is talking in a different language

and when they blend together it
becomes a language you can understand
and may learn to speak at home since
English hasn't been working as well
as it should lately.

At night you can't sleep but it doesn't
matter when you look over at your wife
who is always the only dream
worth having. So you get out of bed,
walk quietly on the hotel terrace
to see how Athens sleeps. Apartment
buildings are white boxes, their shades
closed, and won't open till dawn.
A motor scooter passes by on the street
below, sounding like a zipper being
pulled up on a pair of pants.
A block or two away a dog barks
with an accent but sounds
more like a hound than Greek.
A few moments later as you turn
to go inside, you glance at the moon
just to see another familiar face
from back home.

Parthenon

When you arrived in Athens
you discovered the Acropolis
was never named after a diner
down on Second Avenue and
the Parthenon could never fit in
your hand the way it always did
with coffee to go in a paper cup.
Your hotel was just blocks away.
At night you sat on the roof staring
at the ancient ruin, lights shining
on it—lit up like an old man
on good wine.

The next day you toured the Acropolis
so amazed you kept taking photos
of the Berilie gates, a few
columns, next the east cella, another
of a blonde in tight shorts. You pick
up a stone to put in your pocket
as a souvenir and to weigh you
down against the wind that kept
knocking your cap off like a bully
from the grammar school near Plaka.
Below the east pediment stronger
gusts blow dust off the ground
spinning it into a statue of Athena
who stares into your face until
another gust blows her away.

In the Acropolis museum
a young statue of a sixth century
boy holds onto a calf that is
draped over his shoulders like
a sweater. You admire him since
you were never able to hold onto
anything for that long in your life.
Near him is a maiden with the kind
of curves in her stone you couldn't help
noticing. Even with her hands missing
along with a bit of nose, she still
looks hot and hasn't put on an ounce
of marble around the hips for centuries.

Outside you stop to look down at Athens
that in the distance under the bright sun
looks like a path made of white pebbles
and beyond it the sea. You decide
to go for a swim and now
that you are convinced it takes more
than one god to run a universe,
you are able to jump up on a wall,
step down on rooftops and stroll
all the way to the Aegean.

3:00 AM

The sound of Fred Astaire tap
dancing woke me. I looked over
at the clock, saw it was 3:00 AM,
rubbed my eyes and realized
it was the sound of raindrops
hitting the tin roof of the cottage
we were renting in Key West.
I looked over at my wife still
sleeping, kissed her shoulder,
got out of bed and walked
out on the deck. I inhaled deeply;
even if I took this air, brought
it to the cleaners back home
and had it pressed and delivered
on a hanger, it would never
smell this clean.

Today was our first on the island
and I'm pleased we have two more
weeks, even happier to hear
temperatures in New York City
reached record lows and snow
down here only means poor reception
on a TV screen. We spent most
of the day on the beach at Fort Zach,
watched schooners sliding out
on the Gulf until they fit into bottles,
pelicans searching for only the wettest
waves, making it easy for them

to smash open and fly away with fish
in their beaks.

After dinner we stopped at a cigar
stand on Duval Street run by a Cuban
woman who spoke very little English
and since I speak just enough to get
by, I was able to buy a few hand-rolled
coronas. I go back inside to get one
come out on the deck again, sit on
a chair, lean back, light up and smoke
the moon.

Key West

Palm trees surrounding our cottage
applaud every breeze that passes through.
Small jets fly low into Key West Airport.
The next one that wakes me is the one
I'll climb up on the roof for, grab
then put it in the empty parrot cage
the owner keeps in the bedroom, train
it not to make so much noise, feed
it crackers since the airlines stopped
serving food, then send it on its way.

Unexpected cool weather came in
off the Gulf. I go across the street
from where we are renting to an old
conch shack that is being rebuilt. I
ask one of the workers who is putting
on a new coat of paint if he could
spare another since I didn't pack any
warm clothes. He looks into his bucket
and figures there is only enough left
over for a small sweater. I wear large—
thank him anyway.

Pregnant women in white dresses
are sails on a schooner leaving
the marina. It passes a cruise ship
that last night with all its lights on
could have been a high rise from Miami
which fell over on its side during

a storm last week and floated all
the way down here safely into port.
Tourists who poured out of it are walking
along Duvall with locals, college
kids and bikers who parade up
and down the street, revving their
engines because they can. All
walking and riding past crowded bars,
restaurants and small stands selling
cigars, just in case they need
another way to watch their money
burn and go up in smoke.

Chickens roam the streets—the rooster
next door whose timing is always
off keeps crowing dawn up at noon.
And the town claims ghosts of the many
writers who lived here like Hemingway,
Frost and Bishop can be seen walking
the streets at night. Perhaps that's why
it feels like home—all three have
been haunting me for years.

The sunsets here are so stunning
they fill Mallory Square with hundreds
of cameras tourists use to shoot
them. If you look close enough
you'll notice orange brush strokes—
makes me think the town council
must have a special effects department
to do repairs on color and clouds.

Each day ends for me on our porch,
gazing at a star right above
the tall palm trees that look
like Vegas showgirls backstage,
ready to go on when the lights
come up at dawn. It is there
every night, the size of a perfect
diamond no one can afford
and too distant to make a wish.
A star worth every bit of sky—
glittering.

My Mother's Clothes

My mother liked to wait
until after dinner and say
to my father that she couldn't
possibly attend some social event
that was coming up since
she had nothing at all to wear.
And my father liked to point out
that she had three large closets
filled with clothes; some outfits
she wore only once or never
at all. She also had enough shoes
for an army or whenever
the Marines needed to go off
to battle in pumps. She would
just stare into her cup filled
with tea the color of a good tan,
until he'd say go out tomorrow
and buy a new dress. Then he'd
reach into his pocket, try
not to smile and say his arm
was arthritic from years
of reaching back for his wallet
to give her clothes money.
And he was convinced after
reading in the paper that
Gimbels department store was
filing for Chapter 11 because
my mom stopped shopping
there six months earlier.

Three months after my father
died my mother bought her last
dress during a heat wave,
and in the middle of tumors
we didn't know were growing
in her stomach. This time
it was my sister who decided
my mother should wear that pink
outfit at her wake. When I
walked into the funeral home
and up to the casket, I
decided she looked great.
The color of the dress was vibrant,
alive and her hair was the color
of the gold coins I would have
paid to bring her back.
I started to think that maybe
she was just sleeping. So
rather than say a prayer I
leaned over and whispered
in her ear, Mom there's a sale
at Bloomingdale's tonight.
But rather than open her eyes,
jump up and say let's go you
drive, she just lay there.
She didn't move.

Boys Can't be Trusted

My niece likes to sit on my lap
every time I visit. When she wants
me to make up a story rather than read
it from a book, she'll say read me a story
from your mouth. I've been quite prolific
with titles like: *The Fir Tree That Wore Imitation
Fur, The Turtle Who Made Calls on His Shell
Phone* and *The Poet Trees in the Fores*t.
My niece likes to hear about boys who get
in trouble, since girls are smarter and nicer.
I decided then to add some disguised
autobiographical sketches. Two favorites
from the Boy Series are: *The Dumb Boy
in Math Class* and *The Boy Who Could Balance
a Basketball on His Finger but Couldn't
Balance His Checkbo*ok. So I was surprised
when she told me about the boys in her
pre-school class. Michael Chicatelli is very
smart and knows everything about dinosaurs.
Paulie Floater has been showing her tricks
on his yo-yo that only he can do and Walt
Wheeler's father is Walt Disney. How could I
tell her this is how it starts, these little creeps
can't even spell their names but already have
lines to get over on a pretty girl. Next they'll
be ringing her door dressed in expensive clothes,
their European sports cars with names no one
can pronounce sparkling in her driveway, and
jewelry they'll want to give her, then kiss

across her neck. I couldn't let these boys get
away with this and later would have to talk to
her father. But until then and since my niece
was still curled on my lap, I began a new story
called: *Why Boys Who Like Dinosaurs, Yo-Yo
Tricks and Say Their Fathers are Famous are
Liars and Can't Be Trust*ed.

Scattered Crumbs

You stop in a café and order
a coffee from a woman a little
bigger than the scones on sale
next to the muffins with icing
the color of snow piled so high
they could close a school. You take
the empty table near the window
with a half empty cup of cocoa
and scattered crumbs looking
the way Santa might leave it
after a snack on Christmas Eve.

You look out, take a sip then sit
still in order to watch the city move.
A bus rattles like dentures in the cold
on its way cross town; a flock
of pigeons near the curb walk on feet
shaped like pitch forks, their heads
moving back and forth—pistons
to an engine even a mechanic could never
fix. A young boy passing them holds
on to his mother's hand and on to
a string tied to a balloon. When it breaks
free he watches it until it is as high
as Chet Baker's voice and begins to cry.
An old woman crossing the street
alone gets angry, begins to yell,
makes a few important points and
by the time she reaches the opposite

corner, wins the argument and smiles.
It's impressive, you think, how quickly
she settled things.

On a whim you get up and head
into the church next door. You could
have sworn it was Catholic
but the saints near the altar look
Lutheran in the shadows and the rest
aren't even Christian, they're marble.
You find candles flickering near the last
pew, place money in the donation
box then find one that doesn't burn
on both ends, light it and pray it doesn't
burn the bottom of an angel's foot
on the wall a few inches above it.

After you get home you start
washing the dishes, then reach for
the towel that looks like the small
Yorkie a woman down the block
walks every day. When it begins
to growl as you dry the first glass,
you decide to finish later, turn off
the faucet, put on your coat, then
pick up the towel again and take
it out for a long walk.

The Cat That Could Fly

The cat we had as kids never
ate the food we gave him.
Instead he hunted the backyard,
grew heavy on sparrow and robins.
When he spotted small birds he'd freeze,
even in August, turn concrete, stone
twitched more, then he'd pounce,
his jaws filled with thrashing wings
as if his mouth was trying to fly
away from his head. The day
he killed a squirrel and left the body
like a dead Cossack at our back
doorstep, our mother's scream
made trees rustle.

At night in winter we heard him
fight other cats; in summer
it was the sound of car tires spinning
on ice. The gash in his forehead never
healed, his ears were shaped like figs.

The day my brothers and I found him
on the side of the road where he was hit
by a car or a truck, we covered him
with leaves and sticks, his eye staring
like the dime at the bottom of my pocket.
When our four-year-old sister asked
why he didn't come home anymore
we told her he ate so many birds

he just flew away. For months
every time she went out to play, she'd
first stop by the door, shield her eyes
with her hands and look up at the sky.

The View from Here

I walk east along 72nd Street
to where it ends and overlooks
the FDR Drive that runs next
to the waves jogging on the East River.
I sit on one of the new wooden
benches that after a year is already
the color of pigeons. I put on a few
pounds but the traffic on the Drive
is still heavier and I would feel
closer to Queens if Roosevelt Island
didn't come between us. Its three
tall smokestacks look like anti-
aircraft guns pointed at sky, in case
terrorists try again. And today
the sky is clear except for a cloud
shaped like a pillow that makes
the Macy's white sale look
dull. I can make out a jet that
is heading for one of the airports
and is small enough to fit in the belly
of a gull standing on a barge.
And when my wife finally arrives
she walks towards me holding
her hands in front of her with all
fingers moving up and down
as if floating on water so I can
inspect her new nail polish. I tell
her it's the color of the tug
built like a bulldog now under

the 59th Street Bridge. She smiles, sits
down next to me, holds onto my
right arm, looks out over the river
and sighs, then helps me the way she always
does, quietly letting her eyes fill with
everything I couldn't possibly fit
into mine.

Acknowledgments

Grateful acknowledgment is made to the editors of the following publications where many of these poems first appeared.

The Adirondack Review: Snow in San Diego, Watching Pigeons Eat the Last Five Years

The Adroit Journal: The Distance Between Fog and Times Square

Boston Review: Breakfast, Magis, From the Roof

Columbia: A Journal of Literature: Santorini

Crying Sky: Poetry & Conversation: The View From Here, The Week the Factory and Pancreas Closed Down

Greensboro Review: Where You Want to Be, Einstein's Hair

Graffiti Rag: The Truth About Paris

Green Mountains Review: Travel

Harvard Review: A Manual for Urban Living

Hayden's Ferry Review: The Lost Saint

Inkwell: Swimming, Apple Spider, While You Are Away, Key West

Iowa Review: When Iowa Was Washed Away with Milk

Jelly Bucket: Milk, The River, Walking Across America, The View From Here

The Ledge: After Rain, Leaning Against August, Breakfast, From the Roof

Light Millennium: Scattered Crumbs

The Louisville Review: If You Want to Drive Rather Than Walk the Rest of the Way Home

Lumina: On Cold Days Like This, Fishing Out the Moon

Memphis State Review: In a Bar on 2nd

Midland Review: Getting By

New York Quarterly: A Christmas Poem

The North American Review: The Unemployed Man Who Became a Tree

Poetry: Directions Through a Changing Scene

Press: My Father's Hands

Rattle: St. Andrew's Head

Red Rock Review: A Few Extra Days

Rockhurst Review: It's Early

3 AM: Grilled Fish

Valparaiso Poetry Review: Capri, Promises

Vermont Literary Review: Camden

The Worcester Review: Flu Shot

The Academy of American Poets published, "Long as a Quart of Milk" as part of its Poem-A-Day on 5/18/15.

Grateful thanks to the following presses where many of these poems first appeared in book form:

La Jolla Poets Press

River City Publishing

New York Quarterly Books

Black Lawrence Press

Special thanks to Julia Weiss

Kevin Pilkington is a member of the writing faculty at Sarah Lawrence College. He is the author of six collections: *Spare Change* was the La Jolla Poets Press National Book Award winner; *Ready to Eat the Sky* was a finalist for an Independent Publishers Books Award; *In the Eyes of a Dog* won the 2011 New York Book Festival Award; *The Unemployed Man Who Became a Tree* was a Milt Kessler Poetry Book Award finalist. His poetry has appeared in many anthologies including: *Birthday Poems: A Celebration*, *Western Wind*, and *Contemporary Poetry of New England*. Over the years, he has been nominated for four Pushcarts. His poems have appeared in numerous magazines including: *The Harvard Review, Poetry, Ploughshares, Iowa Review, Boston Review, Yankee, Hayden's Ferry, Columbia, North American Review*, etc. He has taught and lectured at numerous colleges and universities including The New School, Manhattanville College, MIT, University of Michigan, Susquehanna University, Saint Vincent College. His debut novel *Summer Shares* was published in 2012 and a paperback edition was reissued in summer 2014. He recently completed a second novel and is working on a new collection of poems.